STUDENT AFFAIRS WORK, 2001:
A Paradigmatic Odyssey

ACPA Media Publication No. 42

George D. Kuh
Elizabeth J. Whitt
Jill D. Shedd

American College Personnel Association
Alexandria, Virginia

TABLE OF CONTENTS

ABOUT THE AUTHORS

George D. Kuh is professor of education and associate dean of academic affairs in the School of Education at Indiana University. George has degrees from Luther College (BA), St. Cloud State University (MS), and University of Iowa (PhD). He has worked in admissions and placement, and was on the faculty at the University of Iowa prior to joining the Indiana University faculty in 1976. A frequent contributor to higher education and student affairs literature, his publications include *Evaluation in Student Affairs* (1979), *Indices of Quality in the Undergraduate Experience* (1981), *Understanding Student Affairs Organizations* (1983), and *Private Dreams, Shared Visions: Student Affairs Work in Small Colleges* (1986).

He is the recipient of the Contribution to Knowledge Award (American College Personnel Association, 1986), the Outstanding Contribution to the Literature and Research Award (National Association of Student Personnel Administrators, 1987), and the Outstanding Service to the Profession Award (College Student Personnel Association of New York, 1986).

Elizabeth J. Whitt is a doctoral candidate in higher education at Indiana University. After completing degrees at Drake University (BA) and Michigan State University (MA), Liz worked in residence life at the University of Nebraska-Lincoln and was the dean of students at Doane College. She served as a graduate student representative on the board of directors of the Association for the Study of Higher Education (1986–88). Her research interests include higher education and student affairs administration, organizational theory, and educational policy analysis.

Jill D. Shedd recently completed the PhD at Indiana University with a double major in higher education and educational inquiry. She also received degrees from Northwestern University (BS) and Indiana University (MS). Jill was the director of educational support programs in the Indiana University School of Medicine for 8 years. Currently an instructor in the School of Education at Indiana University-Purdue University at Indianapolis, she is active in educational program evaluation and research.

PREFACE

Not far from Waitsfield in Vermont ski country is Buel's Gore, an unincorporated area that doesn't appear on the state map. Buel's Gore has seven residents, one of whom is 11-year-old Asa Furchgott. One afternoon, a Bostonian on a ski holiday was driving toward Waitsfield and noticed several bull's-eyes. The closer to town, the more numerous the bull's-eyes became until the bull's-eyes were seemingly everywhere—on billboards, on shacks, on trees. At a service station, the Bostonian struck up a conversation with the attendant and asked about the bull's-eyes.

"Oh," said the attendant, "that's the work of little Asa Furchgott. He's always shooting that BB gun of his."

The Bostonian, thinking there might be a profit margin somewhere in trick shooting, asked for directions to the Furchgott house and went off in search of Asa. He didn't have to go far. Soon he came upon a boy on a dirt bike with a BB rifle strapped to his back.

"Are you Asa?", asked the Bostonian.

"Yep," said Asa.

"Let me see you shoot," said the Bostonian.

"Sure," said Asa as he got off his bike.

Asa slipped the BB gun from his arm, raised the gun to his shoulder, and cracked off four rounds, each one directed toward a different tree. Deliberately, Asa walked to the first tree. As he walked, Asa pulled a large black ink marker from his back pocket. When he got to the tree, he drew a circle around the hole made by the BB. After drawing circles around the remaining three holes, Asa turned to the Bostonian, winked, and said, "Nothin' to it."[1]

In most Western societies, seeing is believing. Seeing a bull's-eye suggests the work of a sharpshooter. What is required for us to see a circle with a hole near the center of the circle and conclude that what we see is a bull's-eye? Some previous experience such as observing knive-throwers at a carnival or trick-shooters at a rodeo might establish a frame of reference for interpreting the relationship between circles and holes and concluding they are bull's-eyes.

But what happens if we turn the "seeing is believing" aphorism around? If, for the time being, we adopt the notion that believing is seeing, how might interpretations of our observations and experiences be different? What does a broken window suggest? Vandalism? An accident—was the window in the path of an errant baseball? Or perhaps the owner forgot a key and had to break the window pane to gain entry. Maybe someone less skilled than Asa Furchgott was playing with a BB gun. Or maybe something else happened. Interpretation of experience depends not only on what we see, but also on what we expect to see and what the common frame of reference or world view encourages us to believe—about broken windows, about bull's-eyes, about anything.

This monograph is about believing and seeing, and about the necessity of suspending common beliefs and assumptions about our world and our work so that, like little Asa Furchgott, we can begin to see and, perhaps, behave differently. Through illustrations from the student affairs field and from various other disciplines, the monograph describes for student affairs staff profound changes under way in the frame of reference or world view most persons in Western culture use to understand events and human behavior. We are not able, in a single monograph, to capture all the characteristics and nuances of the emerging world view or to exhaust the range of implications for every area of student affairs. For example, although feminism has had a profound influence on the once-pervasive patriarchical patterns of understanding (Capra, 1983), we have not emphasized feminist contributions to the emergent paradigm other than through a few references sprinkled throughout the manuscript.

We have chosen to focus on core elements of our field—delivery of services to students, student development programming, administration, research, evaluation and policy, and preparation of student affairs staff.

Four general questions are addressed in the monograph:
1. What is a *paradigm* and what is implied by a "shift in paradigms?"
2. What are the characteristics or qualities of the emergent paradigm and how do they differ from the qualities of the conventional, traditional paradigm?
3. What are the core assumptions on which student affairs work is based that must be reexamined in the context of the emergent paradigm?
4. What are the implications for student affairs work of the shift in paradigms and of the emergent paradigm's underlying assumptions?

We hope that by responding to these questions the monograph will help student affairs staff begin to manage the transition from a familiar set of assumptions to what are, at present, unfamiliar ways of making meaning.

OVERVIEW OF THE MONOGRAPH

The monograph's scope is ambitious. A good deal of material is introduced that will probably be unfamiliar to most student affairs workers. We believe these ideas are best assimilated by reading the chapters in turn, particularly chapters 1–3. We will be satisfied if you read them, in whatever order.

In chapter 1, the concept of *paradigm* is defined and the changing nature of the world in which student affairs staff live and work is briefly described. Examples from several fields (physics, psychology, organizational behavior, literature, history, law) are used to document the pervasiveness of the transition that is under way from a conventional dominant paradigm to an emergent paradigm or world view.

In chapter 2, a conceptual framework developed by Schwartz and Ogilvy (1979) is described and used to identify the qualities or patterns of change that seem to distinguish the emergent paradigm from the conventional paradigm or traditional frame of reference. This promises to be a conceptually rich but challenging discussion. Within the limits of our understanding, unfamiliar concepts and terms are defined in the text and in the appended glossary of selected items. In addition, we have tried to provide illustrations that describe what conventional and emergent paradigm assumptions look like in student affairs practice.

In chapter 3, several core assumptions of student affairs work are tested against characteristics of the emergent paradigm. For example, human development is often discussed in student affairs literature as if development were patterned, cumulative, orderly, and predictable (Miller & Prince, 1976; Rodgers, 1983). In the emergent paradigm, some aspects of human development are interpreted as unfolding in a spontaneous, uncontrollable, unpredictable manner. The material presented in this chapter may be disconcerting as some intellectual, emotional, and existential challenges may surface through such an examination.

Next, some implications of the emergent paradigm for using human development theory and the student development concept in student affairs work are presented. The indeterminate nature of development assumed in the emergent paradigm has powerful implications for attempts to systematically design and implement student development interventions. Self-organization theory (Prigogine & Stengers, 1984) is presented as one alternative for thinking about the process of development.

In chapter 5, the conventional paradigm's emphasis on reason and logic is juxtaposed against intuition and *action learning* (Morgan & Ramirez, 1983) to distill the implications of emergent paradigm assumptions for making meaning in the context of student affairs organizations. The cultures of student affairs units are interpreted within the framework of nonorthodox organizational theory, and suggestions are outlined for maximizing opportunities often found in institutions of higher education.

The methodological arsenals (Schroeder, Nicholls, & Kuh, 1983) developed to examine college student behavior are impressive in the context of the conventional paradigm. But characteristics of the emergent paradigm (e.g., indeterminacy and mutual shaping) challenge the utility of analytical methods grounded in "normal science." In chapter 6, the potential for naturalistic inquiry (Lincoln & Guba, 1985) to enrich student affairs research and writing is discussed.

Student affairs preparation programs are firmly ensconced in conventional paradigm assumptions. In the final chapter, recommendations are offered for how faculty and others can incorporate emergent paradigm assumptions in curriculum and other aspects of graduate study.

A complete reference list is presented at the end of the manuscript rather than at the end of each chapter. The previously mentioned glossary and an annotated bibliography are appended; the latter provides a starting point for those who wish to examine in more detail literature describing the forces that create and nurture transitions of pervasive world views.

Anne Huff (1985) suggested a useful tactic for coping with the ambiguities and conflicts inherent in organizations such as colleges and universities that are characterized by uncertain environments and problematic internal controls. Play "what if." That is, adopt a playful attitude and, through daydreaming or brainstorming, imagine possible or likely near-future scenarios. Huff believes that after entertaining a variety of possible situations, one is better prepared to deal with the implications and consequences of what eventually comes to pass.

We invite you to play "what if" with us as you read through our present understanding of the emergent paradigm or world view. In the process, we think you will begin to see more interesting dimensions to your work with students and colleagues. After all, what's the worst that can happen if you choose to interpret student affairs work using principles consistent with the emergent paradigm? What have you got to lose? Play "what if" with us.

NOTE

1. We are indebted to Susan R. Komives for the idea for this story. The facts are stretched a bit to make the point. For example, although Asa Furchgott lives in Buel's Gore, we have no idea if he is a sharpshooter.

CHAPTER 1

THE SILENT REVOLUTION

great quote.

The wisest creature in the lush, green woodland was an owl. Admired and respected, the owl was often visited by other forest animals seeking advice and counsel. One afternoon, after a torrential downpour, the owl was perched on a log near the swollen river bank. The unusually swift current broke the log loose, and both the log and the owl were swept downstream. Many hours later, the river was not much more than a trickling stream, and the owl was grounded on a river bed surrounded by a treeless prairie. The wisdom acquired by the owl through years of forest living was of little use in the prairie. Overnight, the owl's world had changed.
[Source Unknown]

The world in which student affairs staff live has changed also. Many of these changes are obvious—such as electronic mail, satellite communications, microwave cooking, and space travel. In the next decade, significant changes are expected in the demographic characteristics of college students because of the disproportionately higher Black and Hispanic birthrates in the 1970s. In addition, by 1990: (a) half of all students enrolled in institutions of higher education (IHEs) will attend college part-time; (b) half of the students in IHEs will be over 25 years of age; and (c) about half will not live on campus but commute to college (Hodgkinson, 1985). In the future, the nature of students' experience in higher education, both in and outside of the classroom, will be less traditional.

In almost every discipline other more subtle, yet farther reaching, changes are taking place (Howard, 1985; Kuhn, 1970) that promise to have a profound effect on how student affairs staff will interpret and perform their work in the next century. In this chapter, the emergence of a new world view or paradigm that portends fundamental changes in the way meaning is made will be documented. First, the concept of *paradigm* will be defined for use in this monograph. Examples will be drawn from physics, psychology, organizational behavior, literature, history, law, and economics to document the transition from a dominant, conventional world view embraced by Western culture to an emergent paradigm or world view.

1

FROM A CONVENTIONAL TO AN EMERGENT
WORLD VIEW

Few people have the imagination for reality.
—Johann Wolfgang von Goethe

In human development terms, transitions are characterized by changes associated with biological, sociological, environmental, historical, or other phenomena. Transitions may be obvious, or imperceptible to acquaintances even though relatively dramatic, such as a change in one's career aspirations. Some transitions are sudden, others cumulative, but not necessarily orderly (Schlossberg, 1981). Many student affairs staff are familiar with, if not sympathetic to, such interpretations of human development. Less familiar are the transitions that are under way in the manner in which events in the natural world are interpreted.

Some theorists believe that the core assumptions used to make meaning in the world are in the midst of a major shift (Capra, 1983; Ferguson, 1980; Kuhn, 1970; Toffler, 1984), a *metatransition* (Maruyama, 1976). In the words of Thomas Berry (cited in Schwartz & Ogilvy, 1979):

> We are in trouble just now because we do not have a good story. We are between stories. The *Old Story*—the account of how the world came to be and how we fit into it—is not functioning properly, and we have not learned the *New Story*. The *Old Story* sustained us for a long . . . time. It shaped our emotional attitudes, provided us with life purpose, energized action. It consecrated suffering, integrated knowledge, guided education. We awoke in the morning and knew where we were. We could answer the questions of our children. We could identify crime [and] punish criminals. Everything was taken care of because the story was there . . . it [provided] a context in which life could function in a meaningful manner. (p. 1)

According to Capra (1983), the metatransition can be characterized by three themes: (a) the breakdown of a patriarchal world in which the dominance of male-oriented values of objectivity, independence, and rationality is eroding, (b) the certain demise of a controllable international economy and life style based on fossil fuels, and (c) a shift from a world view characterized by a mechanistic paradigm heavily influenced by causal scientism—in which objectivity, control, and linear causality are superordinate—to a world view characterized by a much more complex, relational, and context-bound paradigm. It is Capra's third theme, the shift in assumptions and beliefs about fundamental laws or relationships that explain how the world works, that is the subject of this monograph. When paradigms shift, understandings are markedly altered and, like the owl's experience, one's repertoire of behaviors (such as those on which student affairs staff have come to rely) may require revision.

A Word About Paradigms and World Views

There are numerous levels of paradigms. At the level of a specialized field of practice, such as student affairs, widely held assumptions and beliefs about students or how to deliver services to students may be thought of as a paradigm. *The Student Personnel Point of View* (American Council of Education, 1937, 1949), the Student Development Model (Miller & Prince, 1976), and the intervention cube (Morrill & Hurst, 1980) could be considered paradigms.

At a somewhat broader level, university faculty are purported to share fundamental beliefs that venerate dualism (the bifurcation of human experience into cognitive and affective domains) and cognitive rationality (the superiority of the intellect and reason over other ways of knowing such as aesthetics) (Conrad & Wyer, 1980; Kuh, Shedd, & Whitt, in press). These beliefs are supported by inquiry techniques grounded in positivist or normal science canons (Campbell & Stanley, 1963) including experimental or quasi-experimental methods and reductionistic data analysis. To describe the "reality" of student life, the student affairs literature has relied heavily on such inquiry methods (Kuh, Bean, Bradley, & Coomes, 1986a).

These paradigmatic levels—(a) the specific assumptions governing student affairs work, (b) a broader set of assumptions explaining faculty attitudes about the primacy of intellect over affect, and (c) an even broader set of assumptions and beliefs influencing the creation of and interpretation of knowledge in all fields—make up an all-encompassing set of assumptions and beliefs that denote implicit and explicit views of reality (Morgan, 1980). The meta-theoretical system of assumptions and beliefs, the dominant or conventional view of the nature of the world, is of primary interest in this discussion.

World views "define, organize, and bring order to [our] lives" (Newton & Caple, 1985, p. 163). A world view enjoys broad acceptance in society and becomes a pervasive belief, internalized to the point that it is no longer consciously questioned. A world view is, in effect, "a description of what is and how it is" (Newton & Caple, p. 163). Since the beginning of recorded history, fewer than half a dozen world views have been documented (Mumford, 1956); the latest emerged during the Enlightenment period in the 17th and 18th centuries (Schwartz & Ogilvy, 1979). Prior to the Enlightenment, inexplicable events were often attributed to whims of the gods, mysteries of life, illogicalities, and fate (Perrow, 1981).

Copernicus and Galileo introduced what has become the conventional paradigm in Western culture. Newtonian laws of physics were established, from which expectations were derived for occurrences in the natural world. The belief in the existence of a natural order of things led philosophers and scientists to seek ways to exert control over events and elements in nature. In all fields and disciplines, thinking and development were influenced by the mechanical nature of Newtonian laws and principles. This perspective, first adopted by physical scientists, is now deeply rooted in Western culture. An excellent overview of the evolution of the mechanical model of the world from the Enlightenment to the present is provided by Lucas (1985).

Thinkers and writers in many fields are now suggesting that the conventional paradigm has begun to unravel. One of the best known discussions about this process is Kuhn's (1970) *The Structure of Scientific Revolutions*. In almost every field of study, discoveries have been made or behavior has been observed that challenges the efficacy of conventional paradigm assumptions. When the number of these events reaches a critical mass, a shift will take place in the generally accepted world view or paradigm. The shift to a qualitatively different, emergent world view not only encompasses propositions basic to the preceding conventional world view but also adds new beliefs and assumptions that suggest alternative understandings or interpretations of commonplace events and behavior. Right now, most disciplines and fields of study are between paradigms—between "stories"—as fundamental changes in long-held, basic beliefs and assumptions about the nature of things and the human condition are being experienced. Consider the following examples.

Physics

Because physics was the cornerstone of conventional paradigm thinking, it is particularly appropriate that physics was one of the first disciplines to challenge the Old Story. In Old Story physics, the universe was composed of matter, tiny billiard ball-like particles thought to be the building blocks of the universe. It was assumed that a physicist in a laboratory could objectively study and predict the behavior of matter under varying conditions. One of the earliest challenges to the conventional paradigm occurred in 1927 when Werner Heisenberg proved that when a photon of light is directed toward an electron to observe its movement, the electron is thrown out of its predicted path of movement. The very act of lighting up an electron disrupts the electron's path (Moore, 1966, p. 151). Heisenberg concluded that it was impossible to observe and measure simultaneously the velocity of an electron because the nature of the observation process affects the results.

Numerous other challenges to the alleged laws of the physical universe have been documented. For example, gravity was long thought to exert the same degree of pull, no matter what the weight or mass of an object. Recently it has been posited that a counter-gravitational force (hypercharge) may exist that slows the fall of denser objects. That is, a denser object, such as an iron cannonball, possibly falls more slowly than a less dense object, such as a water drop (Begley, 1986).

Another questionable conventional paradigm belief is that light is made up of particles. Not long ago, scientists analyzed data that suggested that light behaved like waves. As soon as the wave view was adopted, however, new evidence for the particle theory was found. But if light is particulate, it ought to have mass, and then it could not travel at the speed of light, which it of course does (Zukav, 1980). How can this be?

A partial explanation is the principle of complementarity, which holds that matter behaves in two complementary but, at the same time, contradictory ways (Capra, 1983; Bohr, 1958). If we look at matter one way, it seems particle-like; if we look at matter another way, it can take the form of a wave. "It can never be both simultaneously, because one always excludes the other" (Miller, 1985, p. 12). The form matter takes depends on the experimenter's choice of experiments (Zukav, 1980), and on what one chooses matter to be.

There are two lessons here. First, reality is a matter of choice; what we believe is what we see. Second, there is no reality until something is observed (see Figure 1). Put another way, reality is created through humankind's interactions with the natural world, and does not exist independently of an observer (Zukav, 1980). (Remember trying to decide if a tree falling in the forest makes a sound? The principle of complementarity forces us to deal again with this question and, perhaps, provides us with an answer.)

According to principles of quantum physics, at the subatomic level matter does not exist with absolute certainty; rather, matter has tendencies to exist (Gribbin, 1984). This is mind-boggling because our normal sensing of experience is at the macro-level, not the subatomic level. We look at a piano and think, "The piano is a real, tangible object; I can see it, touch it, and hear it. How can it not exist?" But as the materials composing a piano are analyzed (wood made up of fibers, fibers made up of atoms), at the subatomic level, the existence of protons and electrons cannot be predicted

5

"Nothing yet ... How about you, Newton?"

FIGURE 1
Newtonian Science

with certainty. A single particle apparently can exist in two places at the same time (Jonas, 1982). Subatomic particles cannot be captured in their natural state, however. To create particles such as protons and electrons, human beings have to disturb nature. That is, particles come into existence only in high energy particle accelerators when they are observed by scientists. In quantum physics, the natural world is depicted as "a mysterious unbroken wholeness with separate 'parts' that come into existence" (Miller, 1985, p. 81) only when people create them in their minds (see Figure 2).

"Go ahead and laugh, but he's made some amazing discoveries."

FIGURE 2
The one in the hat is the magician

Source: Drawing by Dawes; copyright 1986, Omni Publications International Ltd.

These are challenging ideas with far-reaching consequences. So-called controlled experiments or any kind of human inquiry— whether in physics or the social sciences—cannot be proclaimed objective or free from the values or the influence of the observer. Indeed, the cutting-edge questions being addressed today in physics were common to those of philosophers or theologians a decade ago (Pagels, 1985) and have much in common with theories of perception (Zukav, 1980). In Oscar Wilde's words, "we cannot get behind the appearance of things to [discover] reality. And the terrible reason may be that there is no reality in things apart from their experience" (cited in King, 1986, p. 81).

Predictable outcomes promised by conventional paradigm axioms are being replaced by laws of indeterminacy and probability. "Science is proceeding in paradoxical directions hauntingly similar to those we are observing and hypothesizing for the world of management theory" (Peters & Waterman, 1982, p. 90). "We are headed for what appears to be a new order of things which relies on an image of the complex interconnections of all things; there is a shift in metaphor from a machine-like universe to the hologram-like universe" (Schwartz & Ogilvy, 1979, p. 7).

Psychology

In some ways, the work of conventional paradigm physicists and psychologists was similar; the former focused on experimental data to confirm laws and principles governing the physical world, the latter developed batteries of intelligence, aptitude, and personality tests to predict and control human behavior. However, if physicists cannot observe events in nature without distorting the object of the observation, surely distortion occurs when both the observed and the observer are human (Tranel, 1981).

In conventional paradigm psychology, the focus was on a singular self attempting to master the contrary components of the psyche, including the unconscious; reason and logic were superior to intuition. In the past few decades, psychology has drifted toward more complex, interactive models that acknowledge the utility of multiple, alternative interpretations of human experience (see Looft, 1973). One example is Carl Jung's theory of multiple personality types existing in each person. Jung's work was subsequently condensed by Myers-Briggs to the typology currently popular among student development researchers.

A more familiar interactive model is transactional analysis (TA) in which the self is viewed as tripartite: parent, child, and adult. Rather than assuming that a single self is in control, a transactional analyst tries to determine which self is in control of which behaviors and how the several selves relate to one another.

Both Jung's archetypes and TA are perspectival and relational. They are perspectival in that a person's behavior is best understood by knowing which role (such as that of adult) is predominant at a given point in time, thereby identifying the perspective from which the individual views the world. They are relational in that behavior must also be interpreted with the other roles (parent and child) in mind. In addition to acknowledging a multiplicity of selves (Gribbin, 1984; Howard, 1985; Lucas, 1985), newer theories of psychology emphasize the influence of multiple "open" systems (Bertalanffy, 1968) of social relations (e.g., family, church, neighborhood) and other environmental influences on behavior.

In the emergent paradigm, the human organism is a dynamic, differentiated but integrated whole characterized more by disorder, instability, and disequilibrium than order, stability, and equilibrium (Caple, 1985; Prigogine & Stengers, 1984). To cope with these complex multiple realities, the integration of reason with holistic, nonlinear thought processes (lateral thinking, creativity, humor) is considered necessary (Ferguson, 1980; Guillen, 1984). Seemingly inconsistent or archetypal behaviors—such as cooperativeness and competitiveness, the capacity to use both reason and intuition in sense-making, or masculine (yin) and feminine (yang) tendencies—can and do exist in each person (Capra, 1976).

Organizational Behavior

In conventional paradigm organizational theory, Weberian ideals of efficiency, knowability, calculability, impersonality, rationality, and technical competence are preferred (Clark, 1985). The classical bureaucratic model is based on assumptions of goal-directed administrative behavior (Etzioni, 1964; see also Strange, 1983) and on rational, linear technologies such as Management by Objectives, Planning, Programming and Budgeting Systems, Management Information Systems, and Program Evaluation and Review Technique.

Over several decades, modifications were made to the bureaucratic model to expand the model's capacity to explain behavior in organizations (e.g., human relations management, contingency approaches, open systems theory, idiographic elements, bounded rationality, situational leadership—Clark, 1985). However, orthodox or conventional paradigm organizational theory has been overextended in attempts to accommodate the complexities workers experience in contemporary organizations such as institutions of higher education (Schwartz & Ogilvy, 1979).

Nonorthodox organizational theorists have rejected the basic assumptions of the conventional (Weberian, bureaucratic) paradigm: (a) that organizational behavior is goal-directed, (b) that individual behavior is preference-directed, (c) that sequential events link intents and actions, (d) that reliability is limited only by situational and contingency factors, and (e) that predictability is limited only by current knowledge and technologies (Clark, 1985). What have been considered in traditional organizational theory to be avoidable deviations or pathologies are rather modal organizational behaviors in the emergent paradigm. That is, loose coupling, varied interpretations of reality, lack of consensus about goals, ambiguity, and failure to achieve goals (to name just a few) are characteristics common to an organization—to be expected and exploited, not to be "fixed" (Kuh, 1983b).

In the New Story, institutions of higher education are characterized by organized anarchy (Cohen & March, 1974), idiosyncratic behavior and beliefs indigenous to student affairs "rain forests" (Schroeder, Nicholls, & Kuh, 1983), and culture or "organizational sagas" (Clark, 1972). All emphasize the importance of subjective, phenomenological processes from which meaning in organizations is derived; there is no "real" world (i.e., single reality) to be discovered—only varied multiple realities to be individually and collectively constructed and understood.

Literature

Just a decade or two ago, there was a fairly narrowly constructed definition of what constituted a literary classic. Today, "we have no classics because there are too many classics" (Bouwsma, 1975, p. 209). Bob Dylan, Sesame Street, and Kurt Vonnegut are just as likely to be required reading in college literature classes as are Milton, Shakespeare, and Mark Twain. A plethora of specialized societies and literary magazines encourages authors and poets to experiment and invent new literary forms. Poetry used to rhyme, but rhymes are now "almost embarrassing in a world that does not permit such simple closures" (Schwartz & Ogilvy, 1979, p. 50).

In Beckett's play, *Waiting For Godot*, nothing happens. That is, Godot doesn't show up. It is possible to draw a parallel with Heisenberg's indeterminacy principle—humankind stumbling along in a world guided by serendipity and happenstance rather than by eternal truths and transcendental meanings (Schwartz & Ogilvy, 1979).

Since the 1950s, an increasingly influential group of literary critics, a significant number of whom teach at Yale, has adapted the deconstructionist perspective attributed to the French philosopher Jacques Derrida. To deconstruct text is to pick apart a passage, chapter, or book and to demonstrate that the text refers not to some extratextual reality but rather has several possible meanings. One or more of these meanings usually are in conflict with other interpretations, which renders the meaning of any piece of writing indeterminate (Campbell, 1986). Once again, the indeterminacy principle and the role of the context and of an observer in making meaning surface as important qualities.

Economics, History, and Law

Until recently, scientific progress in most disciplines was defined as the triumph of reason and method over ignorance and superstition. Today, the appropriateness of using the classical scientific method to answer societal questions is under attack (Winkler, June 1985, 1986; Lincoln & Guba, 1985).

Conventional paradigm economics has assumed a "rational man": humans act predictably according to self-interest rationally derived and communicated (Friedman, 1986). Recently, some economists have acknowledged that econometrics and mathematical models based on this assumption have generated unreliable predictions of oil prices and currency exchange rates (Winkler, June 1985). The stock market, commercial interest rates, and consumer behavior are other illustrations of projections gone wrong.

A number of economists have come to the conclusion that human behavior expressed in economic terms is much more complex than once thought; people are reflexive, inconsistent, and do not always weigh costs and benefits before acting. Spending patterns expressed as buying preferences seem to be associated with dense interactions of culture, individual perceptions, available information (Winkler, June 1985)—even the cosmos ("Market Gurus Jolt the Dow," 1986). Evidence of a perspective consistent with the emergent paradigm is the appearance of a new journal, *Economics and Philosophy*, which asserts that an interdisciplinary, humanistic approach to the study of economics is more appropriate than one using conventional social science methods (Winkler, June 1985).

"Social, economic, and institutional forces have as much to do with shaping ... scientific inquiry as do reason and observation" (T. S. Kuhn in Winkler, August 1985, p. 7). For example, some contemporary historians have warned that historians must make sense of situations "in which the choice is not between value-free objectivity and subjective nonsense, but between making value judgements and lying ... For those addicted to neutral, value-free language in historical discourse the question ... is not, [for example] 'Do you want to describe what happened at Auschwitz in value-free scientific language?' It is, 'Can you describe it in such language and be a good historian' " (Winkler, 1986, p. 10)?

Some legal scholars have argued "there is nothing inherently rational, scientific, or neutral about the law. ... Rather ... law is politics in another guise ... riddled with contradiction and prejudice. The classical concept of law, derived in the 19th century, held that the law was a 'quasi-scientific,' formally defined system of rights" (Coughlin, 1985, p. 5). In contrast, legal realists (sometimes called "Crits") have argued that legal reasoning cannot be independent of the personal biases of a lawyer or judge, the social or cultural context of a case, and the inherent contradictions in the law itself. Legal doctrine—to the extent it exists—is indeterminate (Coughlin). One only needs to review the Supreme Court's decisions about sexual relations between consenting adults over the past two decades to obtain evidence of societal influence and contextual variables on the evolving interpretations of what is considered lawful behavior in the United States.

SUMMARY

The beliefs and assumptions that people use to make meaning of their experience are always in transition. In most instances these transitions are subtle and unfold over a relatively long period of time. But at other times, the nature of the ideas that challenge the prevailing view is so radical that these ideas seem discombobulating. That we are in the throes of such a shift right now is confirmed by evidence being accumulated by scholars from almost every discipline.

The comfortable frame of reference characterized by a relatively simple mechanistic paradigm or world view in which objectivity, control, and causality were superordinate is being challenged by an emerging world view characterized by a much more subtle, complex relational paradigm in which behavior has multiple meanings. Student affairs work as an applied field of practice cannot escape the implications of this evolving world view. In the next chapter, some characteristics of the conventional world view or paradigm are contrasted with important concepts in the emergent paradigm.

CHAPTER 2

CHARACTERISTICS OF THE CONVENTIONAL AND EMERGENT PARADIGMS

It is better not to know so much than to know so many things that ain't so.
—Josh Billings, 19th century humorist

If, as the examples from chapter 1 have illustrated, so many beliefs about the world "ain't so," what is so? What does the emergent paradigm look like? The emergent paradigm is not merely a subtle, complex extension or application of conventional paradigm beliefs and assumptions. The differences between conventional and emergent paradigm assumptions are not matters of degree, but matters of substance (Clark, 1985). Old Story and New Story assumptions are not represented by points on a continuum.

In ancient Rome, a two-headed mythical god, Janus, could look ahead and behind at the same time. Janusian thinking—holding two contradictory thoughts simultaneously (Cameron, 1984)—may be appropriate or perhaps the best we can do for the time being. The Old and New Stories are disjunct (Clark, 1985), and a choice will have to be made. We assert that the continually evolving world in which we are living demands a New Story to generate deeper, richer understandings.

Schwartz and Ogilvy (1979) identified seven qualities or patterns of change that distinguish the emergent paradigm from the conventional paradigm (see Table 1). No claim is made that, taken together, these qualities adequately reflect or capture all the characteristics of the emergent paradigm. As we gain more experience with emergent paradigm concepts, perhaps additional distinctions between Old and New Story concepts will be identified. The qualities of the emergent paradigm, as described by Schwartz and Ogilvy (1979), overlap; that is they do not seem to be mutually exclusive. We believe the characteristics of the emergent paradigm will become clearer as we grow comfortable in using them to interpret student affairs work. Nevertheless, for the purposes of this monograph, Schwartz and Ogilvy's work provides a framework within which New Story thinking can be applied to student affairs work.

Table 1
Comparison of Conventional Paradigm and Emergent Paradigm Qualities

Conventional Paradigm	Emergent Paradigm
Student affairs work is . . .	Student affairs work is . . .
Objective Events can be studied from the "outside" with value-neutral instruments and mental processes. *Examples*: objective, value-free data; single truth/reality produced by scientific methods.	*Perspectival* Events are necessarily viewed in light of the viewer's experience, values, and expectations; "believing is seeing." *Examples*: Multiple realities are continually being reconstructed; "multilectic," naturalistic inquiry; hermeneutics.
Simple and reductionistic Events can be explained, controlled, and predicted by reducing them to their simplest components; complexity requires simplification. *Examples*: MBO, PPBS approaches; attrition studies; behaviorism.	*Complex and diverse* Understanding events requires increasingly complex views of their processes and structures; the whole transcends the parts. *Examples*: humanistic psychology; humanistic developmental theory; open systems theory.
Hierarchic Systems are ordered vertically and control, authority, responsibility, and knowledge flow from the top downward. *Examples*: bureaucratic chains of command, formal communication channels, centralization of control over resources and decisions.	*Heterarchic* Order in a system is created by networks of mutual influence and constraints. *Examples*: enrollment management strategies; political model of policymaking in IHEs; clan-like work groups; informal organization.
Mechanical Events are calculable and sequential; actions result in quick and predictable reactions. *Examples*: PERT flow charts; admissions processes, registration, payroll.	*Holonomic* Events are dynamic processes of interaction and differentiation in which information about the whole is present in each of the parts. *Examples*: organizational culture, hermeneutic circles.
Determinate Future states follow from present in rational, predictable ways. *Examples*: human development-stage theories; needs assessments; goal-setting & goal-based planning; single-loop learning.	*Indeterminate* Future events are unknowable; ambiguity and disorder are to be expected, valued, and exploited. *Examples*: loose coupling; "double looping;" garbage can models of decision making & problem solving.
Linearly Causal Events have finite, indentifiable causes. *Examples*: accountability systems; standards and "excellence" movements; problem solving; futurism.	*Mutually Shaping* Events are generated by complex reciprocal processes that blur distinctions between cause and effect. *Examples*: campus ecosystem models; positive and negative "amplification cycles."

14

Table 1 (Continued)
Comparison of Conventional Paradigm and Emergent Paradigm Qualities

Conventional Paradigm	Emergent Paradigm
Assembled Change is planned implementation of prescribed processes that create predictable results. *Examples*: long-range planning, planned interventions to purposefully influence student development.	*Morphogenetic* Change is evolutionary and spontaneous; diverse elements interact with each other and the environment to create new, unanticipated outcomes. *Examples*: self-organization dissipative structures theory; career planning functions evolved out of counseling and placement; nontransferability of programs.

Note. The authors are indebted to Clark (1985) and Schwartz and Ogilvy (1979) for the concept of presenting comparisons under separate headings for conventional and emergent paradigms.

Perspectival, Not Objective

Conventional paradigm social science values objective accounts of the events in the natural world (biological processes and physical laws) and of human behavior. The disciplinary perspectives and inquiry methods used to observe and record phenomena, such as students' development, are assumed to be neutral and value-free. Elaborate statistical models and analytical methods have been developed to describe, explain, and predict behavior. But Heisenberg's principle of uncertainty was the harbinger of a surprising quantum physics discovery: objectivity is an illusion (Capra, 1983). "Our culture, language, and world view affect what we perceive and what we do not" (Schwartz & Ogilvy, 1979, p. 15). The conventional world view influences what we choose to observe and are able to record and what we overlook or consider unimportant as well as what we can understand and what is beyond our sense-making capabilities. Simply put, what is seen depends on who is looking, what that person is looking for, and the context in which the observation takes place.

A basketball game looks, sounds, and feels much different depending on whether the observer is playing, sitting on the bench, officiating, or watching from a balcony seat, or if one has played the game before or is seeing the game for the first time. Even players in the same game do not share the same experience.[1]

Phenomenology reflects one feature of the emergent paradigm. Perhaps the work of Carl Rogers (1951, 1961, 1970) and other phenomenologists (Perls, 1969) may once again be required reading in many education graduate programs. Student affairs staff should entertain the possibility that believing is seeing. What one believes to be true constitutes that person's reality. Do circles drawn around holes in trees constitute bull's-eyes, or are the circles something else (see Preface and Figure 3)?

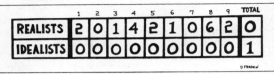

	1	2	3	4	5	6	7	8	9	TOTAL
REALISTS	2	0	1	4	2	1	0	6	2	0
IDEALISTS	0	0	0	0	0	0	0	0	0	1

D FRADON

Drawing by D. Fradon; © 1976 The New Yorker Magazine, Inc.

"Big Bob says he's getting tired of you saying he doesn't really exist."

FIGURE 3
Believing is Seeing

Source: The "Far Side" cartoons are reprinted by permission of Chronicle Features. Drawing by D. Fradon; copyright 1976, The New Yorker Magazine, Inc.

Thus, the process of discovery and understanding will be richer and more fruitful if one uses a combination of perspectives (Kuh, 1984a). A single perspective—whether grounded in a discipline such as sociology or psychology, or provided by a single vantage point in the physical world—can provide only a partial picture of what is taking place. A single perspective or view will always be incomplete in a world that is dynamic and ever-changing. Counseling center intake interviews can never be exact (the principle of uncertainty), nor can such assessments accurately reflect the experience of the same person at a different point in time and certainly not the experience of others. This does not necessarily preclude the existence of an ultimate reality; only that efforts to discover the "truth" will always be incomplete, hindered by our limited ability to muster at any one time the plurality of perspectives needed to capture all the subtleties of a dynamic ecology.

Straightforward questions that are designed to elicit direct responses from among a predetermined set of responses (such as Likert or Guttman scales or multiple choice options typically used on questionnaire surveys), are relatively easy to collate and analyze. But the possible response sets are selected by and are influenced by the inquirer. By determining a priori how respondents can respond, relatively narrow constraints are placed on what can be perceived and ultimately what meanings can be considered important. We will treat this important issue in more detail in chapter 6.

Complex and Diverse, Not Simple and Reductionistic

Those who subscribe to the conventional world view believe that complicated events can be unpacked, explained, predicted, and controlled by using laws or principles discovered by reductionistic, analytical methods. Seemingly complex phenomena can be reduced to understandable elements by aggregating principles into standards for behavior. If one spends enough time and uses the correct inquiry methods, the (simple) answer to any question about human behavior can be discovered. Consider the following illustrations.

Conventional paradigm mathematical and statistical modeling procedures have been used by student development researchers to explain, predict, and suggest ways to control students' behavior. Measures of central tendency and normal distributions are used to portray the reality of students' experience. Student affairs staff experiment to find the correct combination of challenge and support behaviors to encourage multiplistic thinking on the part of dualistic students (Perry, 1970). But if a single reality cannot be captured and constructed through reasoned judgment in a world in which ambiguity, multiple interpretations, and paradox are fundamental conditions of the human experience, how are student affairs staff to behave?

The likelihood of declining enrollments through the mid-1990s is a major threat to the viability of many IHEs. One strategy to counteract decreasing numbers of new students is to do everything possible to increase an institution's retention rate. Therefore, the characteristics of dropouts and ways to reduce attrition are of great interest to student affairs staff and others on college campuses. Retention studies are based on the belief that reductionistic research methodologies can accurately predict who is likely to drop out and what institutional agents can do to increase the likelihood that students with dropout-prone characteristics will persist. In spite of increasing sophistication and power, analytic techniques usually account for no more than 20% to 30% of the variance in attrition. That is, most of whatever is related to students' decisions to leave college has not been detected, despite dozens of published studies. Yet the pervasive belief system suggests we should continue to refine these techniques, the implication being that if we just work harder, add a few more refinements, and sample greater numbers of students and so forth, we can reduce the complexity of the attrition problem to simple answers.

Another example is the principle of in loco parentis, which provided a structure that enabled student affairs workers to impose clear rules on a relatively homogeneous group of students. The rules were plain enough that students knew where they were supposed to be, and what they were to do, at specific times and in various places. Of course, some students failed to comply with such expectations, so elaborate systems of behavior control, such as judicial boards of review, were developed in an effort to respond to deviants. These mechanisms do not necessarily discourage acting out behaviors typical of late adolescents, but they do provide staff with an illusory sense of being in control of the environment.

Despite increasingly sophisticated reductionistic methods, we cannot claim to understand or control human behavior. After reviewing thousands of studies, Berelson and Steiner (1964) came to three conclusions about human behavior: (1) some do and some don't, (2) the differences (between those who do and those who don't) aren't very great, and (3) it's more complicated than that. Similarly, behavior of students, staff, and faculty transcends simple descriptions or predictions and is largly unaffected by attempts to control behavior through simple interventions.

The behavior of students and colleagues eludes simple interpretations because instead of one transcendent objective reality, multiple realities exist. Each person determines for him- or herself the meaning of what is observed. Furthermore, in sometimes unrecognized ways, the context in which behavior is exhibited and the observation process itself influence what is observed or experienced. Capra (1976) suggests that we begin to experiment with ways of knowing other than logical positivist social science methods—such as applying Eastern thought (which emphasizes the basic unity of the elements in the universe) or thought processes that enhance awareness of the mutual interrelations of all things.[2]

The environment in which student affairs staff work is complex and diverse. Institutions of higher education are particularly vulnerable to changes in the external environment that have financial implications (state legislative action, alumni giving patterns, federal financial aid regulations, etc.). These factors coupled with an increasingly pluralistic student body will make student affairs work more complicated in the future. In essence, the world in which student affairs staff must perform cannot be described using a relatively simple model of community living; rather, the college environment is more realistically portrayed as a complex, diverse mosaic characterized by increasing pluralism.

Heterarchy, Not Hierarchy

In the conventional paradigm, hierarchical thinking and behavior are expected, valued, and respected. Expectations for behavior in student affairs units (as well as other societal institutions) are grounded in the premise that the person at the top is in charge and a pecking order exists in control, authority, responsiblity, and knowledge (see Figure 4). As one moves from the "bottom" to the "top" of a student affairs division, the likelihood increases that one can obtain an answer to a question or the solution to a problem (Kuh, 1983a).

In the New Story, heterarchy replaces hierarchy as a characteristic of organizational behavior. Heterarchy reflects "a shift from rule by one to several rules by some" (Schwartz & Ogilvy, 1979, p. 13). In a complex, pluralistic world, no one person is in charge. Relationships with persons on the same level of an organization, or on levels either above or below, are increasingly important to quality decisions, colleagues' morale, and productivity (Kanter, 1983; Peters & Waterman, 1982).

Andrew Grove (1983), the president of Intel Corporation (a high technology firm located in the Silicon Valley), affirmed the importance of heterarchy: "A business like ours has to employ a management process unlike that used in more conventional industries. If people at the top made all the decisions, those decisions would be made by people unfamiliar with the technology of the day. . . . Since our business depends on new knowledge to survive, we [purposefully] mix 'knowledge-power' people with 'position power' people . . . Junior members participate jointly in decision-making meetings with senior managers . . . We don't have any offices, only a maze of cubicles separated by five-foot high sound-proofed partitions. [This is not merely] a visible [badge] of egalitarianism . . . it is really a matter of necessity, a matter of long-term survival" (p. 23).

In a world characterized by complexity and multiple realities, truth or understanding emerge through interactions among per-

FIGURE 4
Old Story Organizing

Source: Drawing reprinted with permission of James Estes; 1986, Phi Delta Kappan.

sons sharing, comparing, and reinterpreting their experience in
the context of others' views. Heterarchy reinforces the validity of
multiple, pluralistic perspectives, holding that different meanings
might be attached to behaviors in an organizational context. For
example, in some circumstances attempts to enlist the cooperation
of staff in other units without obtaining the permission of the supervisor may be interpreted as "an end run" (i.e., ignoring organizational reporting lines). Heterarchical behavior encourages
involvement of more individuals from various places in the organization. Increased involvement, in turn, influences (but not necessarily in knowable ways) certain aspects of the organization and
enhances its capacity to adapt to constantly changing internal and
external conditions. Input from all members of the community is
considered worthy, necessary, and desirable (Ferguson, 1980; Kanter, 1983) to establish and maintain a healthy organizational culture (Schein, 1985). As heterarchical behavior in a division of student
affairs becomes more common, more interactions with more per-

sons in other organizational subunits will occur more frequently. Trust and openness are likely to increase.

At first glance, heterarchical behavior may seem similar to soliciting input of those involved in the context ("stakeholders"), not a particularly innovative recommendation. Indeed, some organizational development specialists have long argued for consensual decision-making modalities. The emergent paradigm implies something qualitatively different, however, than decisions reached through group processes with democratic overtones. More powerful vehicles are needed for testing and interpreting realities than Delphi techniques or quality circles. In chapter 5, some nascent thoughts in this regard will be shared.

Holonomic, Not Mechanical

In the Old Story, the world was thought to function like a giant machine. Every action had a predictable reaction or was connected to some other action. Every question had an answer. When a lever was pushed, the response was almost immediate and usually predictable. For some tasks, a mechanical model is appropriate. Imagine the consternation if the bursar's office failed to routinely send out and collect tuition bills, or if the treasurer's office failed to provide payroll to faculty and staff in an accurate, timely manner.

But a complex heterarchical world—such as that of the student affairs worker—is not usually characterized by calculable, sequential actions. The actions and reactions of students and colleagues are difficult to comprehend or predict fully, let alone anticipate.

In the New Story, the hologram replaces the machine as a guiding metaphor. A hologram is a photograph, taken with a lensless camera, where the whole is represented in all the parts, a record of a dynamic process of interaction and differentiation whereby information is distributed throughout an organism or institution. "If the hologram is broken, any piece of it can be used to reconstruct the entire image. Everything is in everything else; just as if we are able to throw a pebble into a pond and see the whole pond and all the waves, ripples, and drops of water generated by the splash in each and every one of the drops of water produced when the pebble strikes the water" (Morgan & Ramirez, 1983, p. 2).

Holonomy connotes a universal property of nature within the emergent paradigm: a picture or characterization of the whole is somehow contained in each of the parts of the whole (Capra, 1983) (see Figure 5). Examples of holonomic-like phenomena include meditation—attainment of a psychological state in which an in-

"Mr Whalen, is that you or your hologram?"

FIGURE 5
Mirroring Reality

Source: Drawing by G. Cullum; copyright 1986, Omni Publications International Ltd.

dividual experiences unity with the universe (Capra, 1976) and Pribram's (1977) brain theory—information is distributed throughout the brain so that damage to one part of the brain does not always result in loss of memory (i.e., the whole is in the part).

If we extend this metaphor to student affairs, we can see that the character of an institution, or division of student affairs, is contained in, or reflected by, each staff member. This does not imply that student affairs units or individual staff members know everything that is happening in other units or that they can exert control over events in other parts of the organization. Rather, holonomy implies that staff members' intuition and cumulative experiences with students and colleagues are part of a web of understanding that incorporates and transcends unit reports, staff meetings, and any one person's observations or interpretations. Yet, at any point in time, any staff member can describe in general terms, for example, some aspect of the student culture. This description will be generally accurate and thematically consistent with what might be discovered using more formal inquiry methods. But at the same time, to be certain that the institutional portrait adequately represents the institutional mosaic and that this mosaic accurately reflects all stakeholders, every student or staff or faculty member must be allowed an opportunity to have his or her perspective considered. We will return to this point again in chapter 6.

In the emergent paradigm, the context in which a student affairs worker must perform is characterized by an interconnectedness—a stream of interactions among people, events, the institution's environment, and society. Until recently, state-supported institutions had the autonomy to establish new degree programs; today, every state has some form of state coordinating or regulatory agency with varying degrees of control over institutional programs (Millard, 1976). What faculty at one State University of New York (SUNY) system school do is connected in some manner to faculty at other SUNY schools. As a guiding metaphor, holography intimates that everything in a complex open system (Bertalanffy, 1968) is somehow interconnected and that the vision each individual holds is considered legitimate and contained in the whole.

Indeterminate, Not Determinate

According to Cohen and March (1974), coping with ambiguity is the greatest challenge facing university administrators. In the emergent paradigm, ambiguity is a natural quality to be acknowledged and appreciated. Ambiguity can cause problems, of course. Some think that ambiguous situations are a product of ineffective management. Those who expect order and direction sometimes become frustrated when circumstances seem to require action but the ambiguous nature of the situation obfuscates the appropriate action to take. But ambiguity can also be an advantage. Ambiguity permits multiple interpretations so an individual can see what he or she expects or wants to see. Ambiguity allows multiple-choice options in a decision context; staff can decide what tasks are interesting and worth pursuing or whether what they are doing is appropriate. Because ambiguity is pervasive in IHEs, becoming familiar with emergent paradigm concepts can be useful in dealing with some of the paradoxical situations encountered almost daily in IHEs.

For example, students' satisfaction is reportedly related to retention (Astin, 1977). Consider the paradox in attempts to increase college students' satisfaction in order to increase retention. If we are successful in encouraging higher levels of satisfaction on the part of students, the potency of some of the more developmentally powerful challenges students encounter during college may be reduced. Having well-trained residence hall assistants available to help students deal with difficult situations sounds right; but expecting students to work out problems without an institutional agent close at hand may be more consistent with the personal development goal of higher education. If the college provides a challenging, and perhaps more developmentally powerful experience, some students may choose to attend another institution or leave college altogether.

Another paradox. A popular innovation in the 1970s was streamlined course registration, achieved by computerizing the process. This all but guaranteed students courses of their choice because officials could maintain a running tally of course subscriptions and add additional sections of rapidly filling courses. On some campuses, students could register for classes without leaving their residence hall room if they had a microcomputer that could communicate with the mainframe in which the registration records were maintained. The advance computer registration process usually replaced the mass fieldhouse registration event that had a carnival-like—if sometimes frustrating—atmosphere.

In addition to providing an opportunity for the sometimes hysterical campaigning by members of campus clubs, mass registration enabled students to renew acquaintances with peers they did not typically see during the academic year and to talk informally with faculty advisors about such things as course sequencing and career choices. For some faculty, fieldhouse registration (or the mass, in-person registration counterparts) was one of the few times during the year that they visited with colleagues from other departments. Most important, fieldhouse registration was one of the important ceremonies of a college or university—the start of a new academic term. Paradoxically, perhaps in the name of efficiency and student consumerism, many colleges and universities have done away with an important socialization experience.

In a dynamic, indeterminate world, simple reductionistic models or decision strategies will be increasingly difficult to justify as we recognize that uncertainty and paradoxical choice options are commonplace; we must learn to appreciate and value those qualities. Acknowledging indeterminacy does not necessarily render a student affairs staff member impotent to take responsibility for her or his own behavior, or to attempt to influence the behavior of others. Indeterminacy does not intimate fatalism or nihilism. Value-driven choices do influence the outcomes of events and interactions, but not always in knowable or understandable ways, the point which we take up next.

Mutual Shaping, Not Linear Causality

Student affairs staff—as well as most other people—have been socialized to believe in linear causality. *Post hoc ergo propter hoc*;

24

if B follows A, then A must have caused B (see Figure 6). For example, a change for the better in sense of floor community is attributed to the presence of a new resident assistant. In cognitive development terms, students who exhibit conventional patterns of moral reasoning should be encouraged to reflect on their thinking; through confrontation and reflection, students will move to a higher level of moral development.

"Take a close look, and you'll see conclusive proof of my theory that Presidents are named after cities."

FIGURE 6
Post Hoc Ergo Propter Hoc

Source: Drawing reprinted with permission of Chuch Vadun; 1986, Phi Delta Kappan.

According to Kounin (1983), however, "good subjects" do certain things under experimental conditions they would not do in the real world; that is, experiments have their own props and induce certain kinds of behavior in subjects and experimenters. Acknowledging that an experiment shapes the behavior of subjects suggests that different conclusions might be drawn from studies of student development in which interviews are used to collect the data. For example, is it possible that the interviews conducted by William Perry (1970) triggered or encouraged what was subsequently recorded as intellectual development, development that was attributed to or caused by the college experience per se? In other words, does the very nature of the interview process induce certain kinds of behavior on the part of both the interviewer and the interviewee? (Recall Heisenberg's discovery that the act of measurement influences the object being measured.)

An institutional agent's expectations about what students should and should not do, and students' expectations for their own behavior, may account for what is perceived to be a higher level of development. The influence of an interviewer or counselor or faculty member or residence hall advisor does not diminish the importance of what happens to students during college. Student affairs staff, however, must remain cognizant of the possibility that the interactions between a faculty member or residence hall director and a student may encourage unintended and unrecognized behaviors from both student and institutional agent that influence how each behaves and interprets the meaning of the other's experience.

Facts do not have an existence independent of a particular theoretical or contextual framework. Inquiry does not discover the laws of learning and make them known to the inquirers; rather laws and facts are constructed by investigators to create plausible accounts of context-bound phenomena to which they choose to attend (Scarr, 1985). To illustrate this point, Scarr cited research reporting statistically significant correlations between children's IQ scores and measures of parental control; that is, mothers with high control scores tend to have children with high IQs. From some theoretical perspectives (e.g., behavioral), such findings might suggest that discipline influences IQ. But if different facts are introduced, the conclusions may shift markedly. When mother's IQ and education are considered, it turns out that mother's IQ accounts for more variance in child's IQ than any other variable. Mother's IQ also correlates highly with other variables, particularly positive discipline techniques. Is it possible that the child's IQ encourages mother to use positive discipline techniques, not that the discipline techniques employed have a certain influence on child's IQ? Which is cause? Which is effect? (Cunningham, 1986).

In a world characterized by mutual shaping, feedback influences behavior, but in reciprocal, complex ways. Anticipated feedback or specific expectations for certain kinds of behavior may influence behavior. At worst, such interactions resemble a closed system or circle in that when negative behavior is emitted, a negative response is observed ("you shouldn't have done that"). Sometimes different, more desirable behavior is exhibited, but the conditions under which the debilitating behavior cycle is broken are not always clear. At best, a symbiotic relationship can be forged in which individuals' behavior is mutually reinforcing and satisfying. The causes or reasons for qualitatively different responses are impossible to determine. Indeed, what causes certain behaviors may be a meaningless question in the new order of things.

Campus ecology models as they have been presented in the student affairs literature (Banning, 1975, 1980) do not reflect the nuances of the emergent paradigm. However, one of the fundamental premises of the ecology model, mutual shaping, is cause for optimism. Physical structures, aggregated characteristics of students, one person's behavior or expectations, an institution's culture, and other factors continuously swirl and interact one with another, creating an ecological system. If the campus ecology model is interpreted in the framework of the emergent paradigm, no two individuals are influenced in exactly the same way because each responds to the environment in unique, complex, and qualitatively different ways; but each also shapes the environment with his or her behavior.

Morphogenesis, Not Assembly

In the Old Story, the pervasive metaphor for "change is that of a construction project" (Schwartz & Ogilvy, 1979, p. 14). Conventional paradigm assumptions suggest that organizational structures, curriculum, and residence hall interventions to encourage students' development can be "assembled" in an orderly, sequenced manner and will produce predictable, desirable outcomes. Although rarely defined as such, these activities may be considered "closed systems"; that is, each residence hall and each program in a residence hall is independent of and physically isolated from other programs and living units.

Student affairs literature is replete with examples of needs assessments, developmental goal-setting, and sophisticated intervention strategies and programs designed to encourage students to behave in certain ways. For example, a familiar conventional paradigm response by student affairs staff to students' abuse of alcohol is to design and implement an alcohol education program. Another example is the cooperative internship program with local employers to demonstrate to students (and their parents) that college courses do have some relationship to the real world of work. But if the human experience is characterized by diversity, heterarchy, holonomy, indeterminacy, and mutual shaping, we must reconsider whether efforts to exert control and bring order to what is essentially an evolving, unordered experience are a wise use of energy and time.

Morphogenesis is the natural formation and differentiation of structures evolving out of what can be described as chaos; "it is the sense of order emerging from disorder . . . if a system is complex—composed of diverse elements that interact by mutually causal and indeterminant processes—and the system is open to external inputs, then it can change morphogenetically" (Schwartz & Ogilvy, 1979, p. 14). A new form, unpredicted by any one or combination of its parts, can emerge simultaneously.

All biological and social systems are open systems (Sawada & Caley, 1985); open systems maintain themselves by exchanging energy and matter—including information—with the systems in the surrounding environments (Campbell, 1982). Open systems— a student, a financial aids office, a college or university—have histories and are constantly evolving through mutual shaping interactions with other systems—students interacting with peers, faculty, and parents; financial aids office staff interacting with office colleagues, admissions staff, prospective students, and loan officers from local banks; and agents representing the institution communicating with alumni, prospective students' parents, state legislators, and so forth.

To get a sense of how open systems change morphogenetically, three evolutionary states of open systems have been posited: "(a) at equilibrium with respect to its environment, (b) near-equilibrium with respect to its environment, or (c) far-from-equilibrium with respect to its environment" (Sawada & Caley, 1985, p. 14). To picture the differences between the three states, consider the evolution of a hypothetical institution of higher education.

Imagine a small college with an applicant pool just large enough to maintain an annual incoming class of 250. Over a period of years, each entering class numbers about 250 and the size of the faculty and student body remains stable. Assuming adequate alumni support and a steady state economy, the college is a system in ecological equilibrium. If the number of qualified applicants increases modestly, the college must move to near-equilibrium (e.g., hire a few additional faculty, obtain housing for a few more students). But if applications increase dramatically (perhaps due to favorable publicity in the popular press such as *Money Magazine, New York Times*, and *U.S. News & World Report*), the college's system may be pushed to a far-from-equilibrium condition.

At this point, open systems do strange things. The college may quickly add a vice president for external relations, more than a few faculty, one or more permanent residence halls (some high rise units?!?), a host of new courses and several new major fields of study, new departments, a new fieldhouse, and so on. The small college, once at equilibrium with its environment, is now subject to dramatic reordering. Systems capable of this kind of reordering are called "dissipative structures" (Prigogine & Stengers, 1984; Sawada & Caley, 1985).

Systems approaching a far-from-equilibrium condition do not necessarily undergo spontaneous change. At some indeterminate point, however, fluctuations in procedures and policies may become so frequent that change does occur; this critical juncture is called the *bifurcation point*. Neither the bifurcation point nor the characteristics of the reordered state, such as a new organizational structure or the constitution of a faculty governing body can be predicted. The National Aeronautics and Space Administration (NASA) was created for the purpose of space exploration and was at equilibrium or near-equilibrium with its environment. As space exploration became more common and civilians were invited to participate in expeditions, a bifurcation point was encountered. NASA was forced to contend with issues such as passenger safety and insurance, issues more like those that concern travel agents and common carriers (e.g., airlines) than those routinely addressed by space agencies (J. Chancellor, February 26, 1986, NBC Evening News).

Career planning functions evolved out of placement or counseling functions. Some of the reasons for the evolution were common across institutions (e.g., to help students and alumni cope with a depressed economy and contracting job markets for college graduates in certain fields); other environmental factors were institution-specific (e.g., counseling center staff wished to spend time on therapy with individual clients rather than interpret vocational interest batteries with groups of students).

The current forms and functions of NASA or career centers could not have been predicted. In this sense NASA and career centers evolved morphogenetically. Change processes characterized by morphogenesis have profound implications for understand-

29

ing how individual students develop as well as how organizational structures assimilate innovation and evolve. We will address these issues in chapter 5.

SUMMARY

The conventional world view—the assumptions and principles most people in Western culture use to make meaning—is in transition. As with an individual's development, a world view is always in transition. The present transition is more dramatic because a critical mass of observers from virtually every discipline seems to agree that the natural order of things can no longer be adequately represented and understood using the familiar metaphors of machines and construction projects. Rather, the institutions in which student affairs staff live and work, and the systems with which IHEs must exchange energy, are better understood as complex, ambiguous, unpredictable, and often paradoxical. Such an environment is more accurately described as a dynamic, interconnected ecology with mutually shaping elements constantly changing morphogenetically.

But here's the rub. The assumptions on which most of us rely most of the time to make sense of our experiences are not compatible with a dynamic world in which control, certainty, and an objective, single reality have been replaced by conditions of uncertainty, mutual shaping, and multiple realities. Like the once-wise owl whose rich experience living in a lush green woodland is not very helpful in the prairie, student affairs staff will have to rethink the assumptions on which their work is based, and learn new ways of making meaning and behaving. We begin that process in the next chapter.

NOTES

1. Recall the sixth game of the 1986 National Basketball Association championship series played in Boston between the Celtics and the Houston Rockets. Larry Bird led all scorers and played an all-around outstanding game; Rockets star Ralph Sampson played poorly. Did Bird and Sampson "see" or "experience" the same game? Only in one sense—they were both on the Boston Garden court at the same time. But most other claims that Bird and Sampson shared the same experience that day would be difficult to sustain. Would the experiences of Bird and Sampson have been different if played elsewhere, on the Rockets home court in Houston perhaps? Probably.
2. Eastern thought and mysticism seem to capture some of the qualities of the emergent paradigm that we have had difficulty expressing. Yin and yang are opposite tendencies inherent in nature and, some believe, in individuals also. That is, the natural world is characterized by paradox and inexplicable happenings that can be best appreciated by acceptance and marvel. We think that much of what is encountered in student affairs work has similar characteristics.

CHAPTER 3

A REEXAMINATION OF CORE ASSUMPTIONS IN STUDENT AFFAIRS

The longing for certainty and repose is in every human mind. But certainty is generally illusion and repose is not in the destiny of man.
—Oliver Wendell Holmes, Sr.

The propositions compatible with the emergent paradigm are disjunct with those undergirding the conventional paradigm or Old Story. Therefore, the core assumptions and beliefs about student affairs work in colleges and universities must be reexamined. In this section, five assumptions, illustrative of those on which student affairs work is based, will be analyzed within the framework of pertinent features of the emergent paradigm. This discussion may be disconcerting because some fundamental beliefs and assumptions about student affairs work are difficult to defend in the context of the emergent paradigm or world view. These challenges to the ways we think about and do our work will be emotional and existential as well as intellectual.

Reflecting on early quantum physics discoveries, Heisenberg recalled late night discussions with other scientists that ended almost in despair; "At the end [of one of the discussions] I went alone for a walk. . . . I repeated to myself again and again the question: can nature possibly be so absurd as it seemed to us in these atomic experiments?" (Heisenberg, cited in Capra, 1983, p. 76). Einstein's experience was similar: "All my attempts to adapt the theoretical foundation of physics to this [new type of] knowledge failed completely. It was as if the ground had been pulled out from under one, with no firm foundation to be seen anywhere, upon which one could have built" (Einstein, cited in Capra, 1983, p. 77).

Many student affairs staff may have similar reactions to what follows. We can find some solace in knowing that theoreticians and practitioners in most other fields are struggling intellectually and emotionally to respond and adapt to the emergent paradigm.

Assumption #1: Human development is patterned, cumulative, orderly, continuous, and predictable (Miller & Prince, 1976; Rodgers, 1983).

We recognize that this assumption, standing alone, does not accurately represent what many student affairs staff believe about college student development. Historical documents such as *The Student Personnel Point of View* (American Council on Education, 1937, 1949) and the Tomorrow's Higher Education Project (American College Personnel Association, 1975) emphasize that individual differences among students are to be acknowledged, even celebrated. Furthermore, students develop at different rates, with certain dimensions or *vectors* (Chickering, 1969) being more or less important for each student at a given time.

Although we do not quarrel with such statements, they take the form of espoused principles (student affairs staff say they believe in the concept of individual differences and in responding according to students' different developmental needs), not behavior typically exhibited by most student affairs staff. That is, despite acknowledging different rates of students' development, most developmental intervention programs reflect the assumption that human development is patterned, orderly, and predictable, and, therefore, controllable to some degree. This is not to demean student affairs staff for ineffective use of extant theory or philosophy. Other professionals have difficulty as well in applying theory in practice (Argyris & Schon, 1978). After all, theory does not purport to model reality but only claims to explain events or behavior under ideal conditions. It seems, however, that many student affairs-sponsored programs may be grounded in an assumption about human development that is no longer accurate.

More to the point, what if development is not patterned, cumulative, orderly, and predictable, as has been implied by mechanical models of behavioral science inquiry? Caple (1985), Howard (1985), and Lucas (1985) have argued that psychological constructs grounded in the conventional paradigm will have to be reconsidered in the context of self-organization theory. In the self-organization theoretical framework (Caple, 1985), development proceeds morphogenetically from a state of undifferentiated chaos to a state of articulation, a reordered or reintegrated whole able to function adequately, sometimes better than the organism in the previous state. In the self-organization paradigm, the sense of self emerges through an evolutionary process resulting from reciprocal, mutually shaping interactions with other systems in the environment. On the surface, this seems compatible with the dominant paradigm process of differentiation and integration described by Sanford

(1962), a process sometimes described as first-order change. First-order changes may be those aspects of development that seem to be patterned or orderly such as movement between positions in the Perry scheme (e.g., dualism, multiplistic, relativistic) and the sequence implied by the order of vectors presented by Chickering (e.g., a sense of competence must be attained before a student can focus on managing emotions, followed by clarifying purpose and so on).

Accepting the premise that human beings (students) and organizations (student affairs units) are dissipative structures, however, is a critical departure from conventional theory (development is patterned and orderly, differentiation is followed by integration). Dissipative structures (organisms, humans, IHEs) are open systems that have a tendency (perhaps a drive or need in conventional terms) to evolve toward disorder out of which a new form or order is derived. This process, second-order change, can sometimes take the form of spontaneous self-organization. In conventional paradigm language, we have come to call both first- and second-order change, *development*. Most research and writing about human development in student affairs literature, however, have focused on first-order change—the somewhat patterned and orderly characteristics of human development described by stage theorists. Very little is known about changes of the second order, characterized by spontaneous, systemic evolutions with implications for reordering some aspects of a student's personality (see Table 2).

Intentional interventions in the form of balanced or matched degrees of challenge and support from an external source (other open systems such as a residence hall advisor or career counselor) are not necessarily direct antecedents to evolutionary change in a dissipative structure. The individual (or division of student affairs) has the capacity to evolve or develop without prompting by external forces. This does not mean that the college environment does not influence a student's development. Open systems theory (Bertalanffy, 1968) requires an exchange of energy (Prigogine & Stengers, 1984); that is, students must interact with environmental elements or other persons to evolve. Any influence others exert, however, is not causal in a linear sense. All elements of the environment, including roommates, friends, professors, teammates and so forth continually shape each other in ways that cannot be clearly predicted, controlled, or even—in some cases—understood. The amalgamation of these influences—or none of them—may be related in some manner to the onset of a bifurcation point, which signals the beginning of a transformation in the individual.

Another critical difference between conventional interpretations of the human development process and self-organization theory

Table 2
Comparison of Selected Conventional and Emergent Assumptions About Student Affairs Work

Conventional	Emergent
Human development is continuous, patterned, orderly, predictable, and cumulative.	Some features of development (first-order development) seem to be patterned and orderly. Other features (second-order development) evolve morphogenetically and are spontaneous and unpredictable.
Interventions (programs, educational materials, etc.) can be designed to intentionally facilitate development.	Development cannot be systematically influenced by external events or actions; mutual shaping by environments and people is acknowledged.
Interventions can be transported—with modifications—for use in other settings.	Circumstances peculiar to a particular context or behavior setting preclude use of interventions across settings.
Student affairs organizations are composed of interdependent units and personnel driven by rational, goal-directed processes.	Behavior in student affairs units is usually unpredictable and sometimes arational, idiosyncratic, and decoupled from or inconsistent with espoused organizational goals.
The worth of student affairs contributions to the institution's mission will be acknowledged when student affairs meets the criteria for a profession.	The worth and status of student affairs are judged within the framework of the conventional positivist belief system, a dualistic view that values cognition rather than affect, facts rather than values, academic pursuit rather than nonacademic; positivism precludes equal partnership in the academy for student affairs.

is that, within the latter, the process of developmental change emphasizes the importance of the period of disequilibrium (or the far-from-equilibrium state) rather than the return to equilibrium. In Old Story psychology, development was thought to occur when equilibrium was attained following a period characterized by disequilibrium or dissonance between environmental demands and individual response (the far-from-equilibrium position). Disequilibrium was considered important to understanding development because it provided a point at which a student could move away from, or return to, equilibrium. That is, to attain a position of stability within the environment, instability was necessary.

In self-organization theory, it is not the return to homeostasis that is critical but the period of disequilibrium associated with the bifurcation point, the point at which a reordering or reintegration is required to evolve to a more complex, differentiated developmental phase. The period of disequilibrium is necessarily characterized by anxiety or discomfort of some kind. If the self-organizing model accurately represents development during the college years, efforts to ameliorate challenges (e.g., to enhance retention rates) may be counterproductive to student development.

As with all dissipative structures with open system characteristics, evolution of the self is essentially indeterminate. Although recognizable developmental patterns emerge, these patterns emerge only in retrospect. The details of any pattern always are unpredictable because of the evolutionary autonomy open systems—particularly human systems—possess (Jantsch, 1980). "Chance (randomness) directs the system down a new path of development (second-order change). Once the new path is created (from among many possibilities), determinism and predictability take over again (first-order change) until the next bifurcation point occurs" (Caple, 1985, p. 175). Development is not "dominated by chance alone but represents an unfolding of order and complexity that can be seen as a kind of learning process, involving autonomy and freedom of choice" (Capra, 1983, p. 288).

In this light, fundamental premises (e.g., every student is unique and develops at his or her own rate) of *The Student Personnel Point of View* retain their timelessness and importance. But the exact pattern of development and the disequilibrium-equilibrium process cannot be anticipated, predicted, or directly influenced. Therefore, strategies for working with students to encourage development must be reconceptualized. We will return to the implications of the self-organization theory in chapter 4.

Assumption #2: Student affairs staff can systematically design and implement interventions to intentionally facilitate students' development.

Two corollaries to this assumption are that (a) intervention is preferable to nonintervention, and (b) proaction is preferable to reaction. The expectation that student affairs staff can and should take decisive action to influence specific aspects of students' development is a relatively recent addition to the responsibilities typically assumed by student affairs. *The Student Personnel Point of View* (American Council on Education, 1937, 1949) listed many functions for which student affairs staff might be responsible but stopped well short of suggesting that student affairs staff should take action that might result in students' developing in certain ways.

The concepts of *proaction* and *intentional intervention* surfaced in the early 1970s, after student activism and campus restiveness in the 1960s had prompted an intense reexamination of student affairs purposes and responsibilities. Student affairs staff were often expected to maintain campus decorum, at least with regard to student behavior. Because of this monitoring function, described as reactive in its orientation, staff found themselves occupied with keeping students, institutional agents, and civil authorities from hostile, debilitating confrontations. Such assignments required that staff work long hours with a single purpose: "keep the lid on" or maintain the status quo. The work became increasingly distasteful for many, and leaders in the field attempted to fashion reasoned responses to this dilemma out of which they hoped would emerge more appropriate, more clearly explicated roles for student affairs staff.

Brown's (1972) monograph (*A Return to The Academy . . .*) is often considered the benchmark statement of future role options for student affairs staff. One attractive alternative Brown suggested was that student affairs staff use behavioral and social science research and human development theory to guide their interactions with students. Student affairs work grounded in established theory and research could move closer to the core activities of the academy, and student affairs staff could take on tasks that would be more interesting and satisfying than monitoring student behavior and enforcing the campus judicial code. The concept of student development was tacitly accepted as an appropriate cornerstone for student affairs work with relatively little public debate (Bloland, 1986).

From the early 1970s through the present, the expanding student affairs knowledge base (Bradley, Coomes, & Kuh, 1985; Kuh, Bean, Bradley, & Coomes, 1986a; Kuh, Bean, Bradley, Coomes, & Hunter, 1986) had generally supported the premise that students' development can be systematically facilitated or encouraged through intentional theory-driven interactions with students (Knefelkamp, Widick, & Parker, 1978; Rodgers, 1983). Descriptions of how to conduct rigorous, sophisticated needs assessments appeared (Kuh, 1981c, 1982). This reaffirmed the notions that (a) students' needs could be systematically classified and ranked for priority, (b) that programs to meet students' needs could be designed based on theory or empirical data, and (c) that educational activities could be delivered to students in various settings—purportedly to proactively facilitate students' growth on one or more dimensions.

Developmental programming, several contact hours of structured activity, was based on the assumption that one agent's intervention can direct students' development in predictable ways. Furthermore, such group activities, to be successful, required the condition of readiness on the part of the individual (the epigenetic principle in conventional paradigm terms—Sanford, 1962, the emergent paradigm bifurcation point)—a point reached randomly at different times for each individual. If human development is indeterminate, unpredictable, and characterized as much by disorder as pattern, incrementalism, and order, student affairs staff are not likely to directly influence students' development, particularly through intermittent and relatively brief interactions.

We have no alternative but to reevaluate expectations for proactive, systematic programming designed to induce specific developmental changes in students. Within the context of the emergent paradigm, developmental changes are more likely to be linked to chance (as we have come to know the meaning of that term) than to intention. This is not to say that careful studies will not reveal desired changes within a priori limits of probability. What can never be known for sure is if interventions and development are causally related in the linear meaning of that term. That is, because students participate in orientation, we cannot say with certainty, or even infer, that the orientation event assisted their integration into the academic and social systems of the institution.

As we discussed in chapter 2, the mutual shaping properties characteristic of the emergent paradigm render notions of linear causality obsolete. Students' behavior influences student affairs staff members' behavior, the environment, and the interventions at the same time student affairs staff, the environment, peers and so forth are influencing students' behavior. These influences are not necessarily intentional or purposeful, however, nor can they always be documented or clearly understood; we lack the capacity to completely capture the mutual shaping that is occurring. This does not necessarily suggest that in the New Story student affairs staff are impotent. Action—even action that seems chaotic under the circumstances or uncoupled from extant policy or routine practices—is usually preferable to doing nothing (Weick, 1979). Given the ambiguity that prevails in most institutions most of the time, any action consistent with the student affairs division's purposes and values can usually be justified or rationalized afterwards (Kuh, 1983b). We will return to this point when considering implications for student affairs practice in the next chapter.

Assumption #3: Interventions that work in one institutional setting can be modified for use in another institutional setting.

This could very well have been a corollary to Assumption #2. It is set apart, however, to emphasize the limitations of the conventional paradigm assumption of generalizability and to underscore the importance of the context in which behavior occurs. That is, the meaning of behavior cannot be fully understood or appreciated without understanding and taking into account the context in which the behavior takes place (see Table 2). Sometimes we act as though this were not the case. When presenting programs at professional meetings we often imply (perhaps unintentionally!) that an orientation program developed at old Siwash can be modified for use at Illiana State U. But many student affairs staff have also known for some years that programs cannot be transported from one campus to another (Kuh, 1981b), nor can interventions in one residence hall be implemented in the same way in another residence hall on the same campus with similar results. The students, the staff, the time of the academic year, the weather, and physical surroundings are all different in some ways. These variables are part of the implementation process, a process that differs across sites. Simply put, it is not possible to estimate and then account for, through developmental programming, the possible differences between one student and another, let alone the differences represented in a group of 15–50. Any group intervention is at best a shot in the dark.

Even when working with an individual, human development theory—no matter how well explicated and deliberately applied—cannot account for the range of stimuli to which any one student might respond. How does a staff member know which of the dozens of usable theories available might be helpful at a given moment with any given student? It can be argued that it doesn't make any difference whether the theory adequately captures the developmental status of any given person at one point in time.

Theory can be useful in marking the parameters of behavior considered "normal" or "typical." But, if certain theory-induced parameters are clearly established or too prominent in our minds, they may keep us from seeing something important that does not typically fall within the theory's established parameters, what we usually call normal or typical. In other words, a student's behavior that falls outside a conventional paradigm theory's parameters may be overlooked entirely, or inappropriately interpreted within the conventional theoretical framework.

Some have attempted to address this problem by encouraging those who wish to use theory in their work to ground the theory with the target group (e.g., students on a residence hall floor). Grounding the theory—seeing if the theory's propositions have face validity when applied to the target group—is a useful technique but does not adequately respond to emergent paradigm challenges. Theory is useful for thinking about our work. But we have seen that theory that leads practitioners to expect mechanical, linear processes will always be insufficient for directing practice. Thus the indeterminate, diverse, and interactive nature of human experience precludes interventions that have expectations for outcomes similar to those observed in another setting, despite the best intentions of student affairs staff.

Assumption #4: Student affairs divisions should operate as rational, goal-driven organizations composed of interdependent units and personnel.

Contributors to the student affairs literature (e.g., Borland, 1983; Foxley, 1980) generally describe organizational behavior that is consistent with classical, bureaucratic assumptions. For example, staff activities should be directed by consensually validated institutional goals and student affairs division objectives (e.g., encouraging students' development). No wonder many staff experience dissonance when they observe behavior that seems idiosyncratic or self-serving rather than consistent with a division priority. Because we have been taught to expect rational, data-driven decisions, it is not surprising that staff become rankled when they perceive decisions to be arational, political, and counter to one's own biases (Allan & Jenkins, 1980), expectations, or preferred interpretation of reality. Kuh (1981b, 1983a, 1985) has discussed in more detail these and other questionable assumptions about behavior in student affairs units.

Management by Objectives, Planning Program and Budgeting Systems, and other bureaucratic technologies will continue to be useful for technical processes over which control can be exerted (e.g., payroll, certain budgeting functions, recording of grades, class and physical space scheduling). Expectations that rational, linear planning and decision processes should drive all behavior in IHEs are incompatible with certain organizational theory formulations that embrace emergent paradigm qualities of heterarchy, indeterminacy, morphogenesis, and mutual shaping. To develop richer understandings of behavior in human systems that are continually reorganizing, interpretive frameworks consistent with emergent paradigm qualities are necessary. We devote more attention to the application of emergent paradigm assumptions to organizational behavior in chapter 5.

Assumption #5: After satisfying requirements for recognition as a profession, questions about the worth and status of student affairs in the academy will be irrelevant.

Numerous contributors to student affairs literature have addressed the field's perpetual identity crisis (Appleton, Briggs, & Rhatigan, 1978; Fenske, 1980; Penney, 1972; Stamatakos & Rogers, 1984). Status questions usually focus on perceived shortcomings in (a) appropriate training (i.e., terminal degree in appropriate discipline), (b) theory and research specific to the field, (c) well-defined standards for entrance to the field, and (d) legal recognition of student affairs as a specialized field of practice (e.g., state licensure) (Stamatakos, 1981). Discussions about whether these criteria can be met (or even if they are worth pursuing) have little meaning without considering characteristics common, yet peculiar to most IHEs.

In many institutions of higher education, particularly large research universities, a pervasive conventional belief system is asserted to be widely shared by faculty. This belief system, which Conrad and Wyer (1980) referred to as the "liberal education paradigm," separates intellectual development from affective functioning (dualism) and devalues ways of interpreting and evaluating educational experiences (King, 1986) that consider as legitimate other sensing modalities in addition to the intellectual (cognitive rationality, Conrad & Wyer). Within this paradigm, reason, fact, and theory (the "Holy Triumvirate") are believed to be superior to all other ways of knowing.

A cursory examination of the goals of student development and the espoused goals of liberal education reveals that both sets of goals speak to the development of the whole student. Student affairs staff and proponents of liberal education seem to be working toward the same ends (Kuh, Shedd, & Whitt, in press). However, because both groups emphasize the importance of the cultivation of social-emotional aspects as well as the development of the intellect, neither group will be readily perceived as credible by a culture heavily influenced by the Holy Triumvirate. Therefore, perceived differences between faculty and student affairs staff are more a function of disjunctive belief systems than differences in professional trappings such as terminal degrees and knowledge base.

Because the superior role attributed to dualism and cognitive rationality—elements of the conventional paradigm—seems to reflect the situation on most campuses, changes in the student affairs knowledge base and preparation standards will have a negligible influence on the status accorded to student affairs in institutions of higher education. The only leverage point seems to be that the turmoil in many disciplines associated with attempts to accommodate the emergent paradigm will at some time encourage faculty to acknowledge the interconnectedness of the affective and intellectual domains (Kuh, Shedd, & Whitt, in press).

We recognize that many faculty colleagues do not privately or publicly subscribe to the Holy Triumvirate, and are supportive of the work of the student affairs division. Yet we also believe that the influence of faculty members' disciplines, particularly in the natural and social sciences, coupled with the demands and reward systems of the faculty role, are likely to preclude becoming well acquainted with the contributions made by student affairs staff to the undergraduate experience. Furthermore, few events or student issues are of sufficient salience to capture and sustain the attention of most faculty. Most discouraging is that for some faculty (folk wisdom suggests that the proportions vary by type of institution, fewer at liberal arts colleges, more at large, research universities), students—a student affairs staff member's primary constituency— are at worst a nuisance and at best a necessary distraction from their real work, research and development.

All is not grim, however. According to the Carnegie Foundation for the Advancement of Teaching (1981), the wall dividing the "scientific" and "humane" cultures in the academy "is being continuously breached; the pattern of intellectual investigation is being rearranged . . . researchers feel the need to communicate with colleagues in other fields. . . . This more integrated view of knowledge . . . will create . . . a climate favorable to [holistic] education" (p. 20). In other words, as the emergent paradigm evolves, perhaps faculty will view the goals of student affairs as being more compatible with the mission of higher education, and will view students' personal development during college as central to the mission of higher education. Reason, fact, and theory will remain important but will represent only one of a number of legitimate systems within which knowledge is produced and meaning is made (Kuh, Shedd, & Whitt, in press). If this rapprochement comes about, it will not likely be a function of any technical adjustments made in the professional preparation, knowledge base, or institutional responsibilities of student affairs staff.

FIRST-ORDER IMPLICATIONS

It is much easier to criticize and find fault with the conventional paradigm than to understand and find applications of the emergent paradigm to student affairs practice. Paradigms shift slowly, in part because the ideas associated with a new world view must be understood and accepted by more than a few observers before alternative assumptions can be developed. As the emergent paradigm continues to evolve, substantively different assumptions and their corollaries will, no doubt, surface for use in student affairs.

As with any fundamental breakthrough, the assumptions undergirding the emergent paradigm will have limited applicability for those who ground their thinking and work in conventional paradigm or Old Story structures, expectations, and assumptions. We have been taught and socialized to think in mechanical, causal terms. We live and work in institutions that rely primarily on constructions of reality supported by conventional paradigm axioms (e.g., prediction and control are valuable). This is apparent, for example, in the renewed emphasis on "value-added," quantitative measurement of the benefits associated with attending college. If the only ends or outputs of college considered appropriate measures of the value of college attendance are easily quantified indices such as income or occupational status, then understanding the process of human development during the college years is not likely to be viewed as useful or important.

Through experimentation with different assumptions (e.g., openness to multiple interpretations), alternative constructions of reality based on emergent paradigm concepts may become more obvious and useful. Because of the dynamic nature of reality, it will be impossible to determine if the difficulty associated with attempts to apply these new assumptions is a function of (a) insufficient understanding of or unusable emergent paradigm assumptions, or (b) incomplete or incoherent constructions of reality fueled by badly interpreted emergent paradigm characteristics.

These are but a few of the hurdles to seeking immediate applications of emergent paradigm thinking to student affairs work. As more persons become acquainted with the characteristics of the emergent paradigm, the implications will become more apparent and easier to understand. The process of attempting to develop richer, more differentiated views of the world may be more important than substantive outcomes such as innovative programming or course revisions in student affairs preparation programs. That is, it may not be the decisions or outputs that become most significant but rather the way in which understandings are created.

SUMMARY

Emergent paradigm challenges to core assumptions will surely modify pivotal philosophical and operational guideposts on which student affairs practices are based. These challenges will be difficult to immediately accommodate, and will generate considerable anxiety and frustration within the field. In the emergent paradigm—specifically self-organization or dissipative structures theory—anxiety and frustration are bellwethers of disequilibrium, and may signal a bifurcation point: evolutionary or developmental change. The emergent paradigm may push us to the edge of another bifurcation point, a period of great unsettledness in the dissipative structure known as student affairs work.

Giving up illusions of control and other conventional understandings while learning to cope with the qualities of ambiguity, uncertainty, and mutual shaping will be difficult. We cannot be certain how a particular student's personality will change during college or what the student will accomplish after graduation. Similarly, we don't know for sure what the next stage in the evolution of student affairs work will look like, although it will be more complex than what has come before. The next four chapters offer some ideas for what to do in the meantime.

CHAPTER 4

IMPLICATIONS FOR USING STUDENT DEVELOPMENT CONCEPTS AND THEORY IN PRACTICE

Every new idea has something of the pain and peril of childbirth about it.
—Samuel Butler

In this chapter, we set forth some tentative emergent paradigm implications for using human development theory and the concept of student development in student affairs work. First, some general observations are offered about how the emergent paradigm may encourage a reconceptualization of the process of development during college years. Then some tactics are suggested for muddling through the transition between conventional notions about using student development theory and student affairs practices that are consistent with the emergent paradigm.

THE USES AND ABUSES OF CONVENTIONAL STUDENT DEVELOPMENT THEORY

Student development theory of the Old Story, conventional paradigm supports the illusion that control can be exercised over what is essentially an indeterminate, unpatterned process. Those who attempt to influence students' behavior through theory-based interventions are forced to oversimplify the complex phenomenon of development in order to understand and attempt to influence development.

Theories can increase our awareness, help organize our thinking, and point to areas that demand attention (Knefelkamp, Widick, & Parker, 1978). In that sense, student development theory can help student affairs staff to anticipate and respond to certain issues that seem to be typical of students at different ages. But student affairs staff must not reify theory.

Theory can become a "pathology of consciousness" (Morgan, 1980) if it obfuscates developmental issues not described by extant theory. Student affairs staff must remain cognizant of the differ-

45

ences between systematic and constrained thinking about students' behavior, between becoming aware of issues that should be addressed and disregarding behavior or development not addressed by extant theory based on the majority experience in higher education. We should be aware that current student development theories may not accurately portray the development of persons of color and from other countries, the physically and emotionally handicapped, and those with alternative sexual preferences, and that theories do not address some of the more important psychosocial issues with which these students must contend (see Table 3).

Table 3
Implications of Conventional and Emergent Paradigm Assumptions About Human Development

Conventional	Emergent
Human development theory describes, predicts, and explains students' behavior.	Human development theory cannot account for or explain all behavior, and its use may exclude recognition of behavior not acknowledged by the theory.
Explanatory power of theory can be improved if more advanced analytical techniques are used to study students.	"Bootstrap" approaches or partial, ad hoc theories of student behavior and development are useful for attempts to account for behavior in a particular setting.
A balance of challenge and support is required for development to occur.	Development results from a variety of mutually shaping events; direct causal influence of challenge or support actions cannot be assumed.

The process of student development is not as orderly or patterned as we have believed. This is not an argument for suspending use of theory or trying to advance understanding of human development via theory-building. Instead, we offer it as a caveat, a warning to avoid the attractive alternative of oversimplifying the very complex process of human development. It is also a challenge, a call to seek new or different meanings and uses for human development theory.

In the conventional paradigm, research and theory were judged to be useful partly to the extent that behavior could be explained and predicted (see Figure 7). In the New Story, theory perhaps can be used to extend our appreciation for the variety of ways that students might behave during the college years, and legitimate behaviors that previously we considered developmentally awkward or inappropriate. For example, might two or three alcohol abuse episodes serve as a bifurcation point, a transition to the next developmental evolution characterized by near-abstinence for the remainder of the college years?

46

"Your aptitude tests indicate that you'd make a good hunter or gatherer."

FIGURE 7
Empirical Validation

Source: Bill Hoest. © 1987; reprinted courtesy of Bill Hoest and *Parade* magazine.

Developing "Minitheories"

Researchers and practitioners should consider working collaboratively in a "bootstrap approach" (Capra, 1983) to building "minitheories" (Weick, 1979). That is, instead of pursuing elegant formulations of how development unfolds during the college years, what may be more useful in the near future is an evolving set of partial, approximate, but mutually supportive propositions about students' development (see Table 3). For example, rather than attempting to recast Chickering vectors of development or Perry's intellectual "positions" in New Story language, we must observe students and experiment with interpretations of student behavior that are consistent with the emergent paradigm. For example, student development cannot be adequately understood if considered separate from development during the rest of the life span. Domains of development (intellectual/cognitive, psychosocial) as conceptual frameworks lose much of their descriptive power if they are treated as discrete. Finally, understanding of students is necessarily limited when development is viewed as hierarchical (moving from developing confidence to managing emotions, then on to

47

clarifying purpose—Chickering 1969; Knefelkamp, Widick, & Parker, 1978) and uniform. Whatever reformulations or new propositions are produced may be more useful if they accommodate relevant emergent paradigm principles.

In the New Story, both the breadth and depth of developmental theorizing will have to increase without the conventional paradigm expectation for generalizability. According to Lincoln and Guba (1985), "if there is a 'true' generalization it is that there is no generalization" (p. 124). This presents a paradox not unlike the principle of complementarity, as was discovered in attempts to track the behavior of subatomic elements (is light particulate or wave-like?); what is seen is directly influenced by the observer and context. Therefore, theories constructed at discrete levels of analysis become nothing more—or less—than retrospective explanations of one person's behavior, the interpretation of which is heavily influenced by the observer—a residence hall director, an academic advisor, a financial aids officer, or a counselor.

Certain characteristics of the emergent paradigm suggest that student development theory must accommodate the variety inherent in our work (e.g., working with individuals and groups reflecting a wide range of ages, backgrounds, aspirations, and needs). A particular challenge to using conventional theory in practice will be to focus *both* on normative samples *and* on individuals. As diversity among students increases, we must emphasize integration and transitional themes explicated by developmental theory—the identity issues of Chickering (1969) and Erikson (1963) and the challenges and growth potential inherent in developmental transitions described by Schlossberg (1981). A renaissance of interest in phenomenology (Rogers, 1951, 1961, 1970) and experiential modalities (Perls, 1969) can be expected as therapists and others in helping fields attempt to respond to the unique, holistic, indeterminate nature of the human experience.

Current constructions of human development theory are imprecise; yet emergent paradigm iterations of student development theory will seem quite "soft," inefficient, and perhaps even muddled in Old Story terms. Some of this will be related to our limited capacity to respond and make meaning of multiple realities *and* to reconcile the perceived paradoxes inherent in the New Story. For example, how are student affairs staff to accommodate and attend to both the dynamic interconnectedness of large numbers of students living on campus and at the same time respond to the needs and wants of a recently divorced 34-year-old Hispanic learner? What can we do to balance the natural but seemingly incompatible notions of continuity and change?

Encouraging Development During College

A conventional premise of development is that an appropriate balance of challenge and support from the environment is required. Schroeder (1986) suggested that students' growth and development can be compared to that of garden plants. To bear fruit and flowers, various plants require different amounts of sun (shade), water, and time to blossom. Students, each one unique, also require differential treatment. We agree on the first part of this premise (each student is unique); we don't believe enough is known about development to be certain when a particular student needs "sun" or "water," or has the characteristics of a saguaro cactus. According to Lincoln (1986), a well-trained biologist does not look at a saguaro and say, "This is a sick tree. It needs a more hospitable environment—water, shade, nutrients." Rather, the biologist says, "This is a new form of tree, one which I have not seen before. I must set aside expectations of leaves, maple sugar, and bark and discover the unique characteristics of this tree! And then I'll take a look at the environment in which this tree seems to flourish, its ecosystem, and try to determine what this tree gives to and gets from the ecosystem."

Conventional research suggests that only about 7% of college students experience significant personality reorganization during the college years (Clark, Heist, McConnell, Trow, & Yonge, 1972). For the overwhelming majority, college is a time to refine values (typically the values imparted by parents and other significant persons) in the context of sometimes different but not necessarily competing value systems of peers.[1] Thus, although it is fair to characterize the college years as a time of growth and development, it is also important to remember that many aspects of a student's personality and sense of identity exhibit themes of continuity over the course of the student's life.

What is the proper way to accommodate the conventional understanding of "challenge and support" if students are open systems, capable of sometimes spontaneous, second-order morphogenetic changes? Will we be able to give up this remnant of intentionality? How will student affairs staff define—even explain—their role in the college community if development is thought of as a product of multiple and mutually shaping influences, processes, and interactions within an ever-evolving campus milieu, not a systematic process susceptible to intentional influences by institutional agents? Then try to explain that development that can be understood only in retrospect!

These challenges reflect the yin and yang of student affairs work, tasks that look infeasible because they require what seem to be mutually exclusive or at least conflictual responses from student affairs staff. On the one hand we have no choice but to embrace emergent paradigm qualities and begin to assimilate these concepts into our philosophy and practices. What is this work about if not caring for and empowering the next generation, encouraging critical, responsible, examined thinking, and expecting morally defensible behavior? On the other hand, giving up familiar guideposts will lead more than a few to an existential crisis.

We believe the emergent paradigm will be found compatible with the noble aims of the student affairs field. We will have to reexamine the process by which we further these aims, however, and find ways to translate emergent paradigm qualities into language and practices that student affairs staff can appreciate and to which they can subscribe. Most important, we must shed the conventional notion that development can be facilitated or somehow engineered, and become conversant and comfortable with the process of morphogenetic, incremental, unpredictable, evolutionary developmental change. This will require great patience and substantial doses of lateral thinking. Toward these ends, we offer six tactics for using premises and concepts—compatible with the student development philosophy—that we think will be useful in managing the transition between conventional and emergent world views.

EMERGENT PARADIGM TACTICS FOR STUDENT DEVELOPMENT STAFF

We make no claim that the following tactics (adapted from Weick, 1985) have been field tested by dozens of student affairs staff and have been found to be effective in practice. All we can say is the few people with whom we have shared these ideas have liked them.

1. Expectations matter; don't adopt them casually. They tend to fulfill themselves.

Remember little Asa Furchgott and the story of the bull's-eyes from the preface?[2] If you drive through a slum and see a group of men standing on the street in the middle of the day, do you think you have observed a bunch of loafers looking for trouble rather than looking for work, or might they be a construction crew waiting for a truck to come by and take them to the next job (Klein & Klein, 1984)? When you are about to meet with a group of first-year students participating in fall orientation, what do you expect to see and hear? Are you expecting insecure, traditional age students, lacking confidence and self-assurance?

Believing is seeing. As Yogi Berra said, "You can observe a lot by just watching." If you expect immature behavior from students, the chances are, if you observe long enough, you will see what you have been watching for. This is not to say that traditional age first-year students will act mature if we just believe hard enough. Nor will all adult learners be socially adept and goal directed. Expectations for certain kinds of behavior, however, even theory-driven expectations, may get in the way of seeing something other than what we expect.

In the emergent paradigm, multiple interpretations of behavior will be characterized by complexity and diversity, and behavior can't be predicted. Conventional theory may prove useful to a degree. But be wary of Old Story labels (interpretations) used to categorize students.

2. Labels are powerful. Impose them with caution and deliberation because they can direct action and legitimate inaction.

"Dualistic thinker." "Preconventional moral reasoner." "Unable to defer gratification." When you read and apply these descriptions to students, what images are conjured up in your mind's eye? These are not necessarily positive descriptions. They describe in conventional terms a student who oversimplifies complex issues, expects every question to have a concrete answer, and responds to whims of the moment without taking into account the consequences.

Frequent and consistent use of labels shows that the field is developing concepts of some utility. Students in preparation programs use these terms to describe undergraduates with whom they work; increasingly these and similar terms are overheard at regional and national meetings. Preparation program faculty and those who have labored so long to generate and disseminate a knowledge base on which student affairs practice can be based should be congratulated; their labors are bearing fruit.

Labels, once applied, however, are difficult to change. Like student affairs preparation programs, once one has established a good reputation, it's hard to lose no matter what happens there. Labels are more pernicious when they are used and applied without confirmable, trustworthy evidence. What risks are taken when a student is characterized as a dualist? How certain can we be that we are correct? How can we know if the student exhibits dualistic tendencies generally or if we happened to catch the student on a bad day? Perhaps the student is nearing a bifurcation point, when such dualistic behavior—if it exists—is about to evolve into something else.

The emergent paradigm demands that we acknowledge uncertainty and the possibility of change. How can we suspend judgments, yet respond appropriately to students' needs?

3. Look for student behavior that confirms your expectations *and* behavior that surprises you.

Student affairs staff must remain open to using tacit knowledge and intuition along with conventionally produced knowledge about student development and student behavior. We must seize opportunities to revise our own "theories in use" (Argyris & Schon, 1978), to use our experience with students to confirm and also to question whether what we see is believable.

Surprises usually catch us off guard, with our defenses down. Perhaps we should let down our defenses more often, set aside the categorical schemas we use to classify students, and open ourselves to appreciate behavior that we have often overlooked (or tried to avoid seeing!) because the behavior has not been valued in conventional terms. Is an undergraduate acting out, immature, or is the student nearing a bifurcation point? Can we afford not to entertain the latter notion?

By confirming expectations and remaining open to unusual, surprising behavior, we are likely to see, experience, and interpret everything students do differently. We don't know that this will necessarily make us more effective (probably won't), but it should make us more interesting and better students of the student culture and the campus ecology.

4. Intention is neither a necessary nor a sufficient condition for development or for encouraging students' development.

We must begin to look somewhere other than to student development—in the conventional sense of that term—for our sense of professional identity. The emergent paradigm forces us to study our reflection in the mirror and conclude, reluctantly perhaps, that the emperor is not wearing clothes, at least not the clothes of intentional student development. With emergent paradigm qualities of indeterminacy, mutual shaping, multiple realities, and morphogenetic change, we cannot justify claims of encouraging or facilitating or promoting students' development. Human systems are open to spontaneous, unpredictable changes. As individuals become more differentiated and complex, in conventional terms,[3] they become increasingly unstable and open to additional morphogenetic evolutions. We can watch it happen, offer counsel and support during what seem to be times of great stress and discomfort; we can even continue to practice "plus one" interventions (they probably won't do any harm).

Paradoxically, intentionality has value. Through purposeful behavior on the part of student affairs staff, a set of shared values is communicated that shapes the environment in unknowable ways. Intentionality permits us to order our lives, to feel as though we are doing something worthwhile—which makes an important contribution to the quality of campus life. In this sense, the purpose of intentionality is not inconsistent with the New Story; the conventional relationship (simple, direct, determinate, causal) between purposeful behavior and expected outcomes must be reevaluated.

5. Assess when conventional student development theory works in your setting and when it doesn't. Build your own ad hoc theories of student behavior.

Because human development is a complex, unpredictable process, it is not surprising that a large number of theory families (intellectual, ethical, and moral reasoning, vocational maturation and career choice, person-environment interaction/campus ecology) has been developed to explain different aspects of behavior. We cannot afford to give up all that we have learned from conventional theorizing and research about students. The literature is too rich to be dismissed. Conventional theory helps us to recognize certain aspects of human development. But theory used too passionately may blind us to other equally plausible interpretations of the same behavior or cause us to focus on certain actions and ignore others that could be more provocative and interesting.

The emergent paradigm emphasizes contextual sense-making and demands that behavior be interpreted within the context in which the behavior occurs. That is, the inducements or perceived rewards for students becoming involved in campus activities at one institution may differ greatly from what seems to work at another college. The unknowable factors that mutually influence students' behavior, faculty and staff behavior, and aspects of the physical and psychological ecology we call the campus are continually interacting in ways that make the process of development different for everyone at an institution and certainly different for students at different institutions.

Each student affairs worker must discover for him- or herself what works. This may sound anarchistic or sloppy. We do not expect that large numbers of student affairs staff will begin, willy-nilly, to create numerous bootstrap theories of student growth and development during college. The axioms of conventional theory and practice are too deeply imbedded in our roles and socialization processes for more than a few staff to experiment with ad hoc patterns. But each student affairs worker should try to approach some situations with a playful attitude, without theory-based plans of action. If you know someone who seems to be successful with such an approach, be nice to them. Watch them closely (but not too closely—you wouldn't want to disrupt what they do by your observations) and try to figure out how they work with students and focus on things that extend common sense or theory-linked understandings about students. Staff who are able to distill creative interpretations by adopting fresh perspectives on the meaning of students' behavior are institutional treasures. Encourage their creativity; criticize and learn from their work if they will share their interpretations with you. Most important, model their behavior if you can, recognizing that what works for them may not work for you.

6. **Accuracy may be less important than animation. Almost any theory will do if it gets you actively involved with students so that you learn more about them. Improvise.**

   Although the emergent paradigm is characterized by indeterminacy and uncertainty, we cannot allow these qualities to influence our work to such a degree that we feel paralyzed or ill-equipped to interact with students in what we believe to be purposeful ways. One of the reasons student affairs has played an important, vital role in the development of what is considered to be the most comprehensive system of postsecondary education in the world is that caring, nurturant, responsible, action-oriented, value-driven people were attracted to student affairs work. We are concerned, however, that some may read this far and conclude that the sky is falling, that it doesn't make any difference what they do on their job or how they interact with students or what kind of preparation student affairs staff have, as long as they are nice people.

   Being nice helps. But being nice and being actively engaged with students where students live, study, and recreate is better. In those settings student affairs staff will get the data they need to develop the contingency, "bootstrap" propositions about student behavior that make some behavior seem less common and more interesting. It matters not whether one is convinced that conventional student development theory works or whether the opposite is true. It is important, however, that staff be with students, encouraging, promoting, facilitating some action or involvement on the part of students to generate multiple interaction patterns among people. Students learn more about themselves, peers, and the campus milieu by taking part in some activity. Staff learn more about how different students behave under different conditions when involved in diverse activities, and perhaps begin to construct propositions about the behavior they observe and share those with colleagues. These mutual shaping properties in turn (or out of turn) shape various aspects of the culture of the student affairs work place, how the division of student affairs is viewed on the campus, and why attending to the quality of student life is important.

Emergent paradigm qualities of heterarchy, complexity, and multiple realities give student affairs staff permission to take risks and improvise when working with students and colleagues. As dissipative structures, students (and student affairs staff) have the potential to move toward a bifurcation point and begin to evolve morphogenetically into persons who are qualitatively different but still very much the same. What we do with and for students will somehow be related to this change—and that's why it is important that we exhibit our preferences and values when we are actively engaged with as many students as possible—but we cannot presume to intentionally make a difference.

SUMMARY

Considerable consternation will probably characterize the period during which student affairs staff become familiar with the qualities of the emergent paradigm and the implications of these qualities for student development work. The emergent paradigm discounts the likelihood that students' development can be intentionally and systematically encouraged or facilitated, whether grounded in conventional or ad hoc contingency theories. Student affairs staff can use qualities from the emergent paradigm that acknowledge that purposeful behavior can mutually shape the environment and students' behavior.

The contributions of student affairs to a high quality living and learning environment are not likely to be dispelled by emergent paradigm concepts, at least not in the long run. It may take some time, patience, risk-taking, and experimentation with the New Story before most student affairs staff become comfortable with using concepts like morphogenetic change processes and bifurcation points when thinking about students' development and how to be of help to students. We have faith that the kind of folks who gravitate to student affairs work are flexible and resourceful enough that they will respond to these challenges with enthusiasm and good humor.

NOTES

1. We don't wish to imply that this is an adequate description of what takes place during the college years. Indeed, we would wish to make the opposite point, that the constraints of the conventional paradigm, which we will examine more fully in chapter 6, have made it difficult if not impossible to see certain kinds of changes taking place in ways most of us have not been able to imagine heretofore.
2. Charles Schroeder tells a story about phenomenological absolutism—believing is seeing (Schroeder, Nicholls, & Kuh, 1983; Schroeder, 1986). Briefly, an anthropologist doing field work in a dense rain forest convinces the tribal chieftain to leave the rain forest for the first time to visit England. After years of living in the rain forest, the chief has become, like others in his tribe, functionally nearsighted. After days of cutting through the vines, the chief and the anthropologist reach the edge of the rain forest and come to a savannah. Off in the distance a heard of water buffalo are grazing. The anthropologist asks the chieftain to describe what he sees. "I see bees," replies the chief. After walking some distance, the anthropologist again asks the chief to describe what he sees. This time the chief says, "I see buffaloes." "But chief," says the anthropologist, "You said a few minutes ago you saw bees. What's happened?" "Magic," the chief says, "has turned the bees into buffaloes."
3. It is difficult to write about development without occasionally falling into usage of conventional terms and expectations for the developmental process. The language needed to describe first-order change, which seems to us to be quite similar to what we have come to know to be the developmental process, and second-order change—spontaneous self-organizing—will give us problems for a time because the concepts seem conflictual.

CHAPTER 5

IMPLICATIONS FOR BEHAVIOR IN STUDENT AFFAIRS ORGANIZATIONS

We are all captives of the pictures in our heads—our belief that the world we experience is the world that really exists.

—Walter Lippmann

In this chapter, we will contrast some emergent paradigm perspectives with Old Story, conventional assumptions about institutions of higher education and student affairs units. Some tactics for experimenting with alternative perspectives in student affairs practice are also offered.

ASSUMPTIONS ABOUT ORGANIZING

We believe that student affairs staff generally share conventional paradigm assumptions about organizations and organizing (Kuh, 1983a). Conventional assumptions include: (a) collective behavior in IHEs is goal directed, individual behavior is preference directed; (b) sequential linkages exist between individual and organizational processes such as decision making and resource allocation; and (c) reliability and predictability of organizational processes are bound only by situational and contingent factors such as knowledge and technology (Clark, 1985). Each of these assumptions will be examined and alternative perspectives reflective of emergent paradigm qualities will be presented.

Goal-Directed Organizational Behavior and Preference-Directed Individual Behavior

A plethora of rational decision-making models and technologies (e.g., MBO, PPBS, PERT) and long-range and goal-based planning strategies suggest that organizations are goal-attaining entities. Business journals abound with articles prescribing how to improve the use of decision-making models. Student affairs literature generally supports the caveat: "If you don't know where you're going, you probably won't get there" (Borland, 1983; Dutton & Rickard, 1980; Foxley, 1980).

Assumptions about goal-directed and preference-directed behavior are based on conventional paradigm beliefs in determinacy and mechanism. Future states are assumed to follow from present conditions in logical and predictable ways; intent supposedly precedes action. Complex activities are simplified by breaking down such activities into more manageable and understandable components (see Table 4). For example, goal-based planning is an attempt to predict and control the future. The future is conceived in terms of measurable outcomes or products represented by goals; the more specific the goals and the more quantifiable the outcomes, the more "achievable" the plan—the more likely one is to "get there."

Table 4
Conventional and Emergent Assumptions About Organizations and Organizing

Conventional	Emergent
Hierarchical structures are normal and necessary.	Heterarchical interactions, uninhibited by hierarchical structures, facilitate organizational learning and effective administration.
Communication channels are clearly delineated.	Information is available from many sources and flows in many directions.
Expertise, control, and authority are vested in and exercised by superordinates.	Any person at any level has the potential to influence organizational behavior in an effective, positive, creative manner.
Goals and means to attain goals are clear, shared, give direction to behavior, and are tied directly to outcomes.	The relationships among events, individual behavior, technologies, and outcomes in IHEs are ambiguous.
Intentions are directly linked to actions.	Intentions and actions, by units or individuals, are loosely coupled, and may, in fact, be understood only retrospectively.
Reliability and predictability of organizational processes are hampered only by factors such as knowledge and technology.	Qualities of indeterminacy, morphogenesis, and holonomy compromise expectations for reliability and predictability.

These assumptions and goal-based planning technologies may be appropriate and effective for certain types of organizations, such as those in relatively stable environments, in which stable ends (production of 100 widgets a day) are linked to reliable means (mechanized widget production line), and in which centralized authority (widget line supervisor) can exert control over syste-

58

matized organizational processes such as widget production (Weick, 1985). Colleges and universities are not stable environments, however.

In chapters 1 and 2, we demonstrated that higher education environments are always in flux and behavior is influenced in myriad ways. In chapter 4, we argued that means and ends of student growth and development are unclear. Control mechanisms in IHEs are fragmented by academic freedom, autonomy granted to professionals, and departmentalization and differentiation of tasks. As a consequence, behavior is shaped by complex interactions with people, time, and events and has remote and unpredictable outcomes. These conditions are inconsistent with rational planning processes and a priori goal statements (Weick, 1979). It is possible that rational planning, when applied to the ambiguous, conflictual environments that characterize IHEs, may have a negative impact on organizational effectiveness. For example, complex and emergent—and, hence, more adaptive—understandings and coping mechanisms necessary for clarifying and making meaning of ambiguous situations are compromised when conflictual ends and uncertain means are oversimplified (Weick, 1979).

Alternative Perspective: Organizational Culture

An alternative perspective for understanding and managing organizations is the concept of culture (Kilmann, Saxton, Serpa, & Associates, 1985; Schein, 1985; Sergiovanni, 1984b)). The cultural perspective suggests that IHEs are held together by processes of sense-making and negotiating social realities. Elements of culture include the ideals, norms, purposes, and traditions that define student affairs work in the institutional context and provide a basis for socialization of newcomers and reintegration of veterans (Kilmann et al.; Sergiovanni, 1984 a,b,c).

The cultural perspective of organizations emphasizes context—the unique requirements a particular setting has for a group of people—and the importance of shared values and meanings (Sergiovanni, 1984b). Many colleges have an "organizational saga" (Clark, 1972), or story about how the college came to be what it is in the present. Within the organizational saga, the norms, folkways, mores, myths, and values that drive the institution can be understood. The saga helps the institution maintain a sense of connectedness between the past, present, and emerging future. Each person within the institution has her or his own version or interpretation of the saga. Decisions about programs, personnel, and admissions criteria are accommodated to the saga—either in advance or in retrospect (Weick, 1979).

Experience has no meaning outside of the specific institutional context in which the experience occurs. Therefore, shared meanings and a sense of identity legitimate or prohibit certain actions. The heterarchical, mutually shaping interactions common to complex, conflictual decision-making contexts (e.g., academic departments, faculty councils, residence hall governing bodies) can encourage and sustain behavior consistent with shared values and commitments (see Table 4). Shared understandings and values generate feelings of security and efficacy under ambiguous conditions by using values to call attention to what activities are important.

Shared understandings may be difficult to imagine or attain in organizations as heterogeneous as IHEs. "Differences among subgroups are greater than values shared in common ... often administrative practices represent the intrusion of one culture on another" (Sergiovanni, 1984b, p. 8). Fortunately, unity of purpose or meaning at the institutional level is not necessary for a student affairs unit to reap the benefits of organizational culture. Student affairs culture can take the form of what Sergiovanni calls "organizational centers" (p. 8), "cultural confederations of compatibility" (Sergiovanni, 1984c, p. 107) with just enough common meanings to create a sense of belonging. A center is a nucleus of beliefs, sentiments, and values that holds a particular group together and provides its members with a sense of identity. The strength and content of culture vary among centers such as academic or administrative units (Department of Anthroplogy, Office of Commuter Affairs), formal work groups within units (Task Force on Academic Dishonesty in the Department of Residence Life), or informal alliances outside the organizational structure (female staff and faculty support group).

Evidence of culture can be found in all parts of a student affairs organization: departmental slogans such as "students are our business" and "do it in the halls"; staff tee shirts; organizational heroes such as a long-time dean of students or the creator of an innovative alcohol education program, or an RA who successfully coped with a student in crisis. Heroines and heroes are role models who represent ideals and values in human form and are important to a healthy culture.[1] Heroes and heroines may be nationally known pioneers in the student affairs field, articulate spokespersons for the contributions of student services to the quality of campus life, charismatic leaders, or unusually creative thinkers.

Rites and rituals translate culture into action and connect the past with the present (Masland, 1985). Many common rituals are not particularly innovative but they are important—such as awards for student and staff achievements, public thank yous for jobs done—as well as jobs done well—beginning- or end-of-the-semester banquets and retreats, informal meetings and coffee breaks, and celebrations.[2]

Whether the concept of organizational culture is consistent with emergent paradigm qualities depends on what one expects to see. A conventional world view perceives culture as a mechanism of control, susceptible to management or manipulation (even for the best of motives) from the "top" of the organization. On the other hand, culture may be viewed as an amalgam of heterarchic and mutually shaping activities—a whole greater and more complicated than the sum of its parts, bonding participants through shared symbols, visions, traditions, and commitments. Within an emergent framework, culture takes on morphogenetic qualities—"management" by sentiment, not goal consensus; integration by affection; motivation by love.

Sequential Linkages Between Individual and Organizational Processes

Sequential links imply that certain means lead to anticipated ends. For example, persons and programs are evaluated to meet perceived expectations for accountability. Orientation of new employees or students ostensibly contributes to their effective adjustment. Procedures, if implemented as designed, should have the desired effects. All these notions assume linear casuality between goals, assembly processes, and ends, which encourage retrospective determinacy (Weick, 1985). That is, the events that occurred are thought to have been caused by specific antecedents and thus are seen as inevitable.[3] Almost always, a direct and causal relationship between or among events is inferred whereas, in retrospect, gaps, obstacles, and false starts are overlooked. We conclude that "rational models work and organizations are tightly coupled systems" (Weick, 1985, p. 113).

Connections between persons, programs, and units in IHEs, however, are of variable strength (Weick, 1985). The links between academic departments and student affairs, for example, may be loose or tight (Kuh, 1983a). Vertical and horizontal management linkages represent varying degrees of coupling. Specific activities may or may not be linked to anticipated outcomes. Events may be as much a product of a confluence of different, seemingly unconnected behaviors as from one set of activities labeled retrospectively as "causes." Communications and information are generally slow to spread. Coordination is intermittent or absent. Processes and activities are evaluated infrequently. Discretion to act is delegated throughout the organization. Decentralization is the norm, if not the rule.

Alternative Perspective: Loose Coupling

Student affairs units may be better understood as systems with variable coupling between or among persons and functions. Coupling is the relationship between or among elements in an organization. If only a few variables or only weak variables are common across units, a system is loosely coupled (Clark, Astuto, & Kuh, in press). The university and its component parts are prototypical "loosely coupled systems" (Weick, 1985) in all the ways just described: coordination, communication, evaluation, and decentralization. Of course, no organization is completely loose or tight. A loose system may be tightly coupled around certain issues or values (e.g., personal growth, religious faith, democracy, academic freedom).

Consider the academic and student affairs divisions at a small college. Regular communication between the two may be limited to information sharing at meetings of division heads; other contacts may be sporadic, prompted by problems (e.g., the need to notify students who must be placed on academic and social probation or to adjudicate plagiarism incidents) or short term responses to special needs (e.g., developing a study skills center, revising the academic advising schedule during orientation week).

There are some advantages to loose coupling. Loose coupling allows units to respond independently to changes in the environment (Weick, 1982) without having to wait for other units to act. Innovation is facilitated because trials can take place in one section of the organization while other units are shielded from the possible effects of failure (Weick, 1976). Loosely coupled systems also have more sensing mechanisms; independent parts interact with the environment, bring in new information, and thereby enhance responsiveness (Weick, 1976). For example, university representatives interact with a large number of external constituents such as local, state, and federal agencies, parents, prospective students, sports fans, business and industry representatives, philanthropists, professional associations, and accreditation agencies. The more varied these contacts, the more complex and interdependent the relationships between the university and its external environment and the more useful the information and understandings that are generated. Finally, loose coupling allows units and persons to take responsibility for their own decisions and activities (Weick, 1982).

Loosely coupled systems also have disadvantages. Perhaps the greatest disadvantage is that some people will feel isolated from other parts of the organization and, as a result, might adapt to priorities of local reference groups in ways that undermine the educational aims of the institution (Weick, 1982). Examples are plentiful in IHEs: recruitment of students without concern for a student's chances for academic success or social integration; detailed financial aid procedures that create obstacles to students' obtaining funds, particularly adult learners and minority students; residence hall staff who become friends with residents and are reluctant to enforce rules. In most cases, none of these behaviors is intended to do harm; it is a matter of responding to immediate needs without acknowledging a more complicated inventory of institutional priorities and needs.

Weick (1982) encouraged administrators in loosely coupled systems to: (a) interpret the unit's diverse activities according to common themes; (b) provide a common language with which people in the organization can communicate; (c) persistently articulate shared visions and commitments; and (d) spend a lot of time with individual participants in an effort to remind them of common purposes and dreams. Although the tasks of a student activities director, hall maintenance coordinator, and financial aid counselor are disparate, commitment to student growth can give those staff members a sense of being part of a common effort and a feeling of connectedness to the student affairs division as a whole. Although we questioned in chapter 4 the appropriateness of linear applications of student development theory, the concept of student development can serve as an important shared belief system that knits together student affairs staff (Oblander, 1986). Other possible themes include campus ecology models and aims of liberal education (Kuh, Shedd, & Whitt, in press).

As an analytical tool, loose coupling has much to offer. Viewing IHEs and the units within them as loosely coupled systems permits greater freedom to question and understand what is happening than does the assumption of tight coupling—or assuming the correctness of tight coupling. Less time is wasted in reinforcing, or attempting to create, sequential linkages; more time can be spent reinforcing what seems at the moment to be working.

Bounded Reliability and Predictability

Conventional beliefs about organizing include the assumptions that reliability of organizational processes is limited only by situational and contingent factors, and that the predictability of organizational processes is limited only by the sophistication of current knowledge and technology (Clark, 1985). Bounded reliability and predictability are manifested in job descriptions, organizational charts depicting communication channels, policy and procedural handbooks, contingency plans, and empirically derived personnel evaluation measures—and in the frustration and confusion that occur when these efforts go awry. These activities assume determinacy, rationality, and a single reality: If one could only make the right preparation/find the right answer/develop the right procedures, problems would not occur and everything would go smoothly. But, "there are no simple answers and there is no simple finite set of causes for anything that happens in an organization. Furthermore, origins are often impossible to discover, because they usually lie at some distance from the symptom and they have usually grown all out of proportion to their beginnings through deviation-amplifying loops" (Weick, 1979, p. 246).

Conditions of ambiguity characterize institutions of higher education. March and Olsen (1976) have described these conditions in more detail as: (a) ambiguities of intention—inconsistent and ill-defined objectives (e.g., conflictual demands of teaching, research, and service for faculty and conflictual priorities of curricular and extracurricular activities for students); (b) ambiguities of understanding—unrelated connections between actions and consequences (e.g., irregular feedback and evaluation processes for faculty and student affairs staff, unclear educational and student development technologies—what works, with whom, and how?); (c) ambiguities of history—no single version of the past exists (e.g., memories are perspectival, and every alumnus has different memories of the same institution; students, faculty, and staff experience a different "college"; budget crises are described differently by trustees than by clerical staff); and (d) ambiguities of organization—participation and attention are fluid and variable (e.g., different issues evoke interest and activity from different persons; the faculty member leading the fight for revisions in the general education component of the curriculum during the fall semester is away on sabbatical leave in the spring; student demands for social freedoms ebb and flow). Under these circumstances, belief in predictability and reliability seems naive, if not futile.

In colleges and universities "administrators and instructors work on variable raw materials with little control over the supply; they have no firm standards by which to judge the impact of their work and no clear theory of causation that specifies the effects of the things they do" (Weick, 1985, p. 119). IHEs have been described as "organized anarchies" because of the ambiguities inherent in their operations (Cohen, March, & Olsen, 1972; Baldridge, Curtis, Ecker, & Riley, 1977). Yet, many student affairs staff exhibit a strong preference for "single loop learning" (Argyris & Schon, 1978), a predilection for oversimplifying the complexities of life in IHEs.

We have assumptions and beliefs about how things are supposed to work—how things should be in divisions of student affairs (Kuh, 1983a). When things don't go as planned or as we think they should, we seek out the problem or error and attempt to correct it. Single loop learning is narrow-minded "error detection and correction in a 'fixed' context" (Morgan & Ramirez, 1983, p. 6).

Alternative Perspective: Organizing Holographically

"Organizing holographically" is to create systems that can learn from their experiences and adjust their structure and activities in response to what they have learned (Morgan & Ramirez, 1983). In a fluid environment, with shifting demands and expectations of society and students, student affairs staff must be sensitive to the external climate and multiple constituent groups. Morgan and Ramirez identify three conditions necessary to encourage such behavior: (a) requisite variety, (b) monitoring and questioning of context and processes, and (c) "minimum critical specifications" (p. 7).

To encourage requisite variety, flexible internal control mechanisms and processes (Morgan & Ramirez, 1983) and "redundancy" or organizational slack (Cohen & March, 1974) are needed at levels in the organization where problems are likely to occur. With redundancy comes flexibility; more actors and more actions are available to respond to needs that arise and increase the likelihood that appropriate actions may be taken. If enough multi-skilled, multitalented people—who are interchangeable to a degree—are available, different tasks can be performed by different members of a work group at different times, thus increasing the variety of job functions. Specialization of functions is counterproductive. At the least, specialists must also be generalists—in general!

Requisite variety permits persons to observe and deal directly with (rather than at a distance from) different kinds of problems. Sources of influence should be localized if possible, and centralized problem-solving committees should be discouraged. That is, if changes are planned, they should be stimulated at the local level—the residence hall floor, the fraternity house, or the financial aid office, not mandated via a directive from the CSAO.

The ability of persons to monitor, question, and find flaws in institutional policies and internal processes is crucial to organizing holographically (Morgan & Ramirez, 1983). Argyris and Schon (1978) call this "double loop learning"—the ability to "challenge and change values, norms, policies, procedures, and 'theories in use' which underlie one's mode of operation." (Morgan & Ramirez, p. 7).

In student affairs work, the enrollment management concept as an institutional strategy (Hossler, 1984) illustrates the importance of holonomic, heterarchical, mutual shaping behavior. Student satisfaction, an index usually associated with achievement and retention, cannot be influenced exclusively or primarily by a college president, a chief student affairs officer, a director of admissions, or a residence hall director. Nor can the provost or an individual faculty member unilaterally identify and implement solutions or mount interventions to increase the quality of student life. Solutions, if any exist, are more likely to surface by working with persons closest to the effective point of action such as resident assistants or academic advisors.

From this perspective, enrollment management transcends a marketing or new student recruitment and retention strategy and becomes an institutional renewal program that involves faculty, students, staff, alumni, and administrators in discovering what makes the institution successful. In an effective enrollment management program: faculty become cognizant of how their disciplines are viewed by prospective, current, and former students; administrators are sensitized to the strengths and weaknesses of the institution as perceived by on-campus and off-campus groups; and student affairs staff learn from students and others what is needed to maintain a secure, pleasant living environment that encourages students' achievement and satisfaction (Kuh & McAleenan, 1986). Hierarchy is out, heterarchy is in!

"Minimum critical specification" (Morgan & Ramirez, 1983, p. 7) is the process of identifying only what is necessary to get an organization, a project, or a task in operation; the appropriate structure must be allowed to emerge. What are the minimum enabling conditions necessary for enhancing a healthy sense of community on a residence hall floor? A floor government? A resident assistant? A programming ideas workshop? A comfortable floor lounge? The minimum critical specifications will vary by floor, by hall, by institution. The point is not to overstructure in advance, but to let the ongoing and evolving needs of the people and the circumstances dictate what happens. Organizations as well as people can be self-organizing; structure develops out of questioning, assessment, conflict, and competition among ideas (Morgan & Ramirez). This process also provides variety and flexibility and, therefore, greater sensitivity to changing needs.

One way to maximize self-organizing—or morphogenetic—qualities is by avoiding negatives (Morgan & Ramirez, 1983). Deciding what the student affairs division will not be or do provides greater freedom in deciding what it will be. Only a few parameters are defined, so that staff can act unconstrained by a priori goals or "shoulds." The aim is to create a system that is not designed to achieve fixed goals or orient itself to a predetermined future state, but one that is continuously self-organizing so that desirable futures can emerge (Morgan & Ramirez, 1983). If the student affairs division does not wish to be known as the campus discipline unit, what can staff do to change the image?

Action learning (Morgan & Ramirez, 1983) is another mechanism for encouraging holographic organizing. Action learning is a form of purposive reflection in which one becomes conscious of one's own values, assumptions, and actions and, therefore, a self-conscious and active participant in creating and negotiating the social reality or culture that is the student affairs division. Action learning is learning to learn—taking a critical but active stance toward experience. Action learners incorporate as many ideas from others as possible in decision making, take risks through experimentation, and are skeptical about what their experiences teach them. They never assume they have discovered the "best" way or "correct" answer—only that what they are doing seems to be working for the time being.

Weick's (1979) prescription for action learning states that "chaotic action is preferable to orderly inaction" (p. 245). This does not mean that unreasoned activity is encouraged. Action, not planning or thinking about doing something, produces learning. Through trial and error and success and failure—learning by doing—we gain understanding about the institution and the student affairs unit, and become better able to generate actions that seem to match the institutional context.

Heterarchic and democratic action learning is consistent with emergent paradigm qualities. Everyone in the organization is believed to have the capacity for reflective action and all are given responsibility for learning and problem solving. In an action learning mode, pluralism is embraced and differences are celebrated, not repressed, in order to promote maximum variety and unconstrained mutual shaping events. By acknowledging the interconnectedness of problems, solutions, perspectives, and circumstances, action learning is a process that integrates understanding at all levels of the organization.

Holograms, action learning, and chaotic action may seem puzzling (if not nonsensical) to minds attuned to conventional paradigm concepts of predictability and reliability. However, sensing direction through variety, action, and involvement of many persons throughout the student affairs division is quite compatible, humane, and even sensible in the ambiguous, loosely coupled context of colleges and universities.

Military metaphors predominate in Old Story thinking about organizations. Weick (1985) offers a new metaphor—surfing—which comes much closer to the ideas and images we are trying to evoke:

> People who surf do not command the waves to appear, or to have a particular spacing, or to be of a special height. Instead, surfers do their best with what they get. They can control inputs to the process, but they can't control outcomes. To ride a wave as if one were in control is to act and have faith. The message of newer perspectives often boils down to that. (p. 134)

TACTICS FOR ORGANIZING

The tactics introduced in this section are synthesized from the work of Clark (1985), Huff (1985), Kuh (1983b, 1984c, 1985), and Weick (1979, 1985). They can be adapted by student affairs staff working at any level of the organization in any size institution.

1. *Adopt a cultural perspective.* Context is everything. Do what you can to understand the values common to the student affairs division and how meaning is made in your unit. The student affairs culture can be rooted in the commitments and values of the field that have been consistently affirmed over the past 50 years (American Council on Education, 1937, 1949; American College Personnel Association, 1975; Council of Student Personnel Associations in Higher Education, 1975). These historical documents and a growing literature base provide a rallying point for staff: holistic development of the student as a unique individual. Seek tight coupling around key visions (e.g., helping students develop life skills) and values (e.g., affirmative action). A loosely constructed—and tentatively held—framework of consistency will help you keep your bearings and provide others with a working knowledge of what's expected, what's reasonable, and what's not.

Adopt broad-based definitions of organizational problems and solutions. Minimize goal-setting and detailed explications of standard operating procedures. Goals can discourage staff from addressing or seeing other potentially interesting and beneficial activities. Pursue symbols rather than goals; symbols provide general notions about valued outcomes but keep criteria for achievement flexible, allowing for creativity, innovation, and responsiveness along the way. Treat goals as justifications for past activities.

Create some melodrama in the pageant that is student affairs work. Highlight heroes and heroines; emphasize community and create opportunities for ceremonies that reinforce connections and commitments and that acknowledge contributions made by faculty, staff, and students. Encourage rites of integration such as holiday parties and birthday celebrations. Expose new staff to "basic training" to acclimate them to "how things are done" in the student affairs division. Because organizational entry and socialization processes are expensive and time consuming, hiring decisions are crucial (Weick, 1982). Ideal job candidates are persons who hold values and beliefs consistent with the unit's commitments and mission but who can also add unique and organization-enhancing skills and views.[4]

Explore your organization's potential as a center or collection of centers. Tell "stories" that demonstrate unit priorities and values. How should the student affairs division be portrayed: as a regulatory agency (in loco parentis) or as a source of innovative programming for the community? Is the financial aids office a haven for bureaucrats or a service-oriented information center? Are student affairs staff viewed by students as energetic and enthusiastic student advocates, workaholics, or spies? Are there unique programs and policies in which staff can take pride and find a sense of identity? What subgroups (e.g., new staff, "old" staff, task-related groups, men, women, "upper-level" administrators, middle management) exist, and do they make positive or negative contributions to shared meanings and values?

2. *Create developmentally powerful environments for people.* Put another way, organize for adults. Focus on the needs, interests, hopes, and dreams of the people who live and work in the student affairs division. Assume that the capacity for reflective action, responsibility, and learning is widely distributed throughout the student affairs division. Share risks as well as benefits. Create opportunities for acquiring broader and deeper skills. Encourage staff to question assumptions and to find flaws in institutional policies and practices, and reinforce their ability to observe, analyze, and develop alternatives to achieve desired ends. Is it necessary to have residence hall staff (Schroeder, Nicholls, & Kuh, 1983)? What if there were no formal student government and students developed their own rules and regulations for behavior?

3. *Think heterarchically.* Define responsibilities broadly and experiment with a variety of tasks; discourage territoriality. Decentralize decision making as much as possible so that the student affairs division can profit from a wide range of perspectives and the quality and sources of information available are maximized. Strive to incorporate the ideas of as many people as possible (particularly those closest to students) in the development of new programs and the reorganization of administrative structures. By participating in decisions, staff will acquire broader knowledge about the student affairs division and will become more valuable to the institution.

Avoid fixed patterns of leadership. Encourage those who routinely take notes and those who convene groups to experiment with different roles in other groups and settings. To respond to constantly changing conditions in the institution, roles can be adapted, modified, and clarified through the natural order of events (Morgan & Ramirez, 1983). Information about the institution and "the way to get things done around here" becomes more widely distributed. Ownership and commitment to the purposes of the institution also are increased.

4. *Think "process."* Be aware of the evolutionary nature of organizations. They are "streams of materials, people, money, time, solutions, problems, and choices" (Weick, 1979, p. 42)—ever moving, ever changing, ever evolving into unanticipated forms. Challenge consistency. Exploit the benefits of loose coupling including autonomy, adaptability and experimentation (Hedberg, Nystrom, & Starbuck, 1976). Relax rules in order to explore alternatives.

Take action. Try leaping before you look. That is, the best way to find out what you are doing and what is working—at least temporarily—is by taking action, not necessarily thinking about it. Behavior is the stuff from which useful information and experience can be distilled and direction and purpose can be discovered.

Trust intuition and distrust memory—it can lead to debilitating expectations and entrenchment of practices and assumptions (see Figure 8). Don't overinstitutionalize programs and procedures that seem to work in one setting. Policies developed for institution-wide implementation are often ineffective when applied in a specific context. For example, a policy that prohibits use of alcohol forces "street-level bureaucrats" (Lipsky, 1980) responsible for enforcing policies, such as residence hall staff, into an untenable position if they observe a minor infraction by a typically well-behaved student engaged in the rite of passage that is "the first beer." Professionals in IHEs, recognized for their expertise, enjoy considerable autonomy. A street-level bureaucrat typically interprets policy to fit the particular context and his or her own preferences and needs.

Acknowledge, appreciate, but don't overemphasize built-in, natural control systems such as individuals' need for order and stability, expectations for working in formal and informal groups that develop norms, routine practices such as payroll distribution, and so on. Intervene sparingly. Concentrate on avoiding negatives; provide minimum critical specifications. Don't overmanage. Conducting an orchestra, advising a student government, or supervising a housing office may be most effective when it is unobtrusive and tacit.

5. *Complicate yourself and nurture organizational complexity.* "Interesting people and interesting organizations create complicated theories of themselves" (March, 1972, p. 123). Encourage complex behavior and understandings. Dealing with a complex,

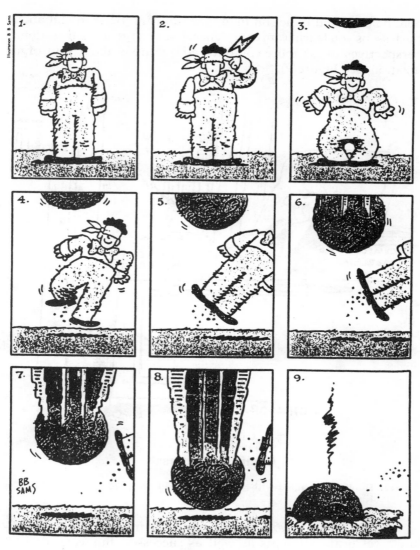

FIGURE 8
Trust Intuition

Source: Drawing reprinted with permission of BB Sams; 1986, Sky Magazine.

heterarchical, mutually shaping world requires complex, heterarchical, mutually shaping activities and sources of information. Avoid fixed patterns of response; think and act in contradictions. Play "what if" (Huff, 1985). For example, plan for both budget cutbacks and increases. Because one can't predict what will happen, be prepared to act on many possibilities. Be skeptical about the lessons you learn from experience. Use emergent organizational perspectives to ask more complicated questions about your organization (see Figure 9).

FIGURE 9
Complicate Yourself

Source: Drawing reprinted with permission of H.L. Schwadron; 1986, Phi Delta Kappan.

6. *Encourage innovation.* Encourage trials and expect failures; celebrate attempts as well as successes. Innovate, daily if possible. Be flexible; not all students or staff have the same needs or perform to their potential under the same circumstances. It is important that student affairs staff be in touch with students and open to learning things about students that may stretch the boundaries of extant theory. The student affairs work environment should not be inhibited by narrowly drawn goals and job descriptions; the culture must be allowed to self-organize, unencumbered by a multitude of rules and policies (Kuh, 1983b).

7. *Be patient; reject quick fixes.* There is no single, simple, identifiable cause for what happens, or how a healthy student af-

fairs culture evolves. Instead, find satisfaction in multiple and partial answers. Expect to have to reaccomplish things. New student orientation, student government elections, and residence hall room assignments are annual events, and each year they must be recreated—as if they are taking place for the first time. Similarly, building a sense of community within the organization, developing an understanding of and a commitment to student development within the student affairs division, teaching faculty and staff what the student affairs division is about, and helping students to understand institutional expectations for behavior must be accomplished over and over again.

Most important, spend time—lots of it—on your job, with students, with colleagues, and reflect on what is important to you and your institution (Kuh, 1985). There is no substitute for persistence, for spending time. According to Cohen and March (1974), persons in a position to devote time to decision-making activities are advantaged for three reasons: (a) they exert influence over the definition of relevant issues; (b) they usually have more information about the issue than anyone else, and as a result they are perceived as more knowledgeable and influential; and (c) they increase the likelihood that they will be present when a decision is made.

8. *Have fun.* Take pleasure in the journey.[5] The positive benefits of humor are so well known that it's disappointing to us that so few people seem to truly have fun on their jobs. Those who laugh at themselves report lower levels of stress, are less anxious, feel more productive, and in general feel better about themselves and their work. People like to work with others who are upbeat, enthusiastic, and seem to enjoy what they are doing. Equally important, these attributes bring on "positive amplification cycles" (Weick, 1979), times when routine events are interpreted in positive and opportunistic ways. Under these conditions, opportunities are turned into advantages, affect is positive, people feel good, and the student affairs culture looks healthy (Kuh, 1983b; 1984c; 1985)!

A Note About Leadership and Strategy

Tactics are minor actions taken to encourage behavior consistent with the values expressed in the organizational saga. Tactics without a guiding vision or strategy are hollow. Vision is not a function of tactics or empirical analysis (Whetten, 1984). Broad-based understanding and support of institutional missions and policies are needed for a healthy, self-organizing division of student affairs to evolve. That is, leaders must be able to play music, not only notes (Pondy, 1978).

Certain basic skills are taken for granted: negotiation and conflict management, group process, knowledge of participative decision models, leadership theories, and planning models. Because leadership acts are as much expressions of culture as anything else, leaders must also be able to evoke understanding through the use of symbols and themes. What a leader stands for may be far more important than what the leader does. Leaders must display integrity at every turn, and consistently articulate and personify the values and principles they hold important. Indeed, principles are far more important than style, technique, and specific tactics. Those who hope to lead must do so by example, by repeatedly articulating and emphasizing key values, commitments, and purposes such as striving to make each interaction with a student a developmentally powerful experience and perceiving themselves as educators (Sergiovanni, 1984a, c).

SUMMARY

Student affairs staff must nurture an organizational culture in which student affairs staff, faculty, and students are able to learn from—yet be ambivalent about or question—their own experience, and—to the extent possible—take advantage of opportunities to mutually shape their environment to reflect what they have learned (Morgan & Ramirez, 1983). These conditions are often systematically maligned in the pursuit of efficiency and scientific management principles.

Emergent paradigm assumptions about organizing may be threatening to those who believe that authority and regulatory mechanisms are necessary to student affairs work. To take advantage of the opportunities for self-organizing in the emergent paradigm, a high tolerance for ambiguity and a sense of playfulness are needed. As we suggested in the preface, play "what if" with us, at least for two more chapters.

NOTES

1. Robert Shaffer was dean of students at Indiana University in the 1960s. The work was particularly trying because of student activism. Bob took every opportunity to affirm the rights of students to express themselves. He led by example: Even though his own son died in Viet Nam, Bob continued to meet and work with students and faculty who protested what they considered to be an unjust war and who challenged Bob's authority as a university official. His visibility on the campus, even during the darkest hours of his personal tragedy, made him a hero in the student affairs division to colleagues across the country themselves beleaguered by student unrest and institutional politics.

Shaffer also championed the value of professional development. Even though his staff worked extremely long hours, Bob insisted they come together on Saturday mornings to discuss a recent book or article. The Saturday morning discussions became a rite of renewal for him and his colleagues (Kuh & Coomes, 1986).

2. Sometimes rituals can be made up. At one eastern college, the need for some guiding force or bonding experience was keenly felt. A creative residence life director decided that a softball game followed by an informal social would be a good way to get the student affairs staff together with the RAs, whose contributions were traditionally unrecognized. He announced the date of the "17th Annual Staff-RA Softball Challenge Extravaganza." Presto! Instant tradition!

3. Reflecting now-passé masculine traits personified in Old Story organizations, attempts to more tightly couple organizations (make communication and decision-making processes functionally interdependent—Weick, 1979) ignore morphogenetic qualities of organizations and inadvertently devalue feminine values (Forrest, Hotelling, & Kuk, 1984) usually underemphasized in institutions of higher education. "The setting and maintaining of boundaries, through organizational flow charts; the institution of single leaders and the resulting emphasis on power and control; the deliberate institution of sameness of ideas and people, and its assurance of suppression of conflict or difference—all these behaviors come from overemphasis and dependence on masculine qualities and denial or suppression of the feminine qualities" (Schaef, cited in Forrest, Hotelling, & Kuk).

4. One way of changing the culture is to attract new staff whose values and attitudes are different from the dominant (unhealthy) culture but that are consistent with the desired culture. This is quite risky, however, as considerable support must be given to newcomers or they will probably begin looking for a different job within months. Focusing so much attention on the newcomers may distract the leader from equally important organizational tasks.

5. The student affairs field has had its share of culture builders; Elizabeth (Betty) Greenleaf was among the more effective. She participated in the development of one of the largest residence hall systems in the world and, with Kate Mueller and Robert Shaffer, was one of the architects of a nationally recognized master's degree program in college student personnel administration at Indiana University. No one worked harder or longer hours than Betty. On the wall in her office hung a large poster made by one of her students that displayed a saying of which she was fond:

Get it done.
Get it done right.
Have some fun getting it done.

CHAPTER 6

IMPLICATIONS FOR KNOWLEDGE PRODUCTION IN STUDENT AFFAIRS

None of the social sciences can predict worth a damn.

—Seymour Lipset
(cited in Winkler, June 1985)

Before we choose our tools and technologies, we should choose our dreams and values.

—Marilyn Ferguson

What we think we know and how we learn what we know are inextricably intertwined. That is, what we believe to be true is influenced by how we obtain the information that supports our assumptions and beliefs. Accordingly, an examination of the implications of the emergent paradigm or world view for student affairs work must consider knowledge production and curriculum in student affairs preparation programs. In this chapter we address the former.

First, some of the limitations of extant knowledge and accepted inquiry methods in student affairs are discussed. The axioms of logical positivism, the preferred conventional paradigm inquiry approach, are compared with axioms of naturalistic inquiry, a methodology consistent with qualities of the emergent paradigm (Lincoln & Guba, 1985). Examples of inquiry activities using the premises of naturalistic inquiry are provided. We conclude with a modest inquiry agenda to illustrate how problems facing student affairs can be addressed through naturalistic research, evaluation, and policy analysis.

Cracks in the Armor of Conventional Paradigm Inquiry in Student Affairs

A well-respected faculty member from the humanities prefaced his comments to an all-university faculty governing body about to consider a controversial proposal with the following:

> Hopefully our work will prove more useful than the findings from the study
> of the bouncing beer can, which held that if you drop a full can of beer and
> you rap sharply on the top of the can with your ring-finger knuckle before
> opening the can, you will get 89 to 94% as much foam splattering all over
> your shirt as you would have if you hadn't done anything in the first place.

Irreverent illustrations like this are not likely to appear in articles published in respectable journals. Yet, a healthy proportion of the research reported in some periodicals—including student affairs journals—is as narrowly drawn and probably as useful as the bouncing beer can study. To the extent that our journals report studies of similar scope and import, it is not surprising that practitioners find these studies of little use in understanding the world in which they work.

Blind allegiance to logical positivism has had an unintended, but pernicious, influence on what can be known about the college student experience and the contributions of student affairs work in the academy. Student affairs workers are in the business of responding to students' needs and shaping the college environment in a manner compatible with the institution's mission. Short, simplistic questionnaire surveys or checklists designed to assess satisfaction with programs or with other aspects of the college experience sometimes generate useful data. But such data fall far short of estimating the importance of the contribution of a staff member who sits up all night with a depressed student or one who meets over the noon hour with a student government officer anxious about chairing his or her first meeting.

Validity and reliability requirements for parametric statistics, grounded in the canons of logical positivism, stipulate that the phenomena under study be normally distributed in the population and that participant variance be homogeneous across samples (Tuckman, 1978). Although nonparametric statistics are available (Siegal, 1956), most studies reported in student affairs journals have used parametric statistics (Kuh et al., 1986a). Requirements for use of parametric statistics have often been suspended in studies of college students. Few colleges and universities have a "normally distributed" student body. Because the great majority of samples used in college student research are drawn from single institutions (Kuh et al., 1986a), most studies probably violate one or more parametric assumptions. Even when most of the assumptions are met, powerful multivariate analytical techniques leave more than half of the variance in most college student behaviors unexplained. When samples are drawn from multiple institutions, such as studies of college outcomes (Astin, 1977), the data are usually aggregated in ways that describe central tendencies or "typical" behavior. Paradoxically, descriptions of everyone describe no one.

If qualities such as indeterminancy, diversity, complexity, multiple realities, and mutual shaping more accurately describe the nature of student affairs work, inquiry methods compatible with these qualities will have greater utility for student affairs. Although the inquiry approaches congenial to emergent paradigm assumptions are of recent and evolutionary development, New Story data will probably be just as good as—if not better than—those gathered in the past for promoting understanding of students' behavior and other human phenomena (e.g, decision making, planning, organizational behavior). The emergent paradigm has the potential to break the grip of "dust-bowl empiricism,"[1] and to enrich both our scholarship and our practice (Kuh, 1981a). In the next two sections, we describe one inquiry approach compatible with the emergent paradigm.

A CLASH OF AXIOMS

We do not intend to provide a primer in naturalistic inquiry and other modes of discovery compatible with emergent paradigm assumptions (e.g., case-study, qualitative, ethnographic, hermeneutic approaches). Those who wish to learn how to conduct naturalistic inquiry are strongly encouraged to consult additional references such as Lincoln and Guba (1985). We offer this admittedly truncated review of the fundamental premises of naturalistic inquiry because they mirror many emergent paradigm qualities with which student affairs knowledge producers should become familiar (see Table 5).

Four axioms of inquiry differentiate logical positivism from naturalism. The first axiomatic difference is ontological, involving assumptions about the nature of reality. According to logical positivism, reality (that is, a single reality experienced by all) can be known, predicted, and controlled. Investigators, using the scientific method, can discover this reality ("Truth"), and, through reductionistic mechanisms, can analyze various aspects of the phenomenon under study (e.g., causes of student attrition). If necessary, pertinent aspects (e.g., student satisfaction, ability, motivation) can be examined independently to learn more about the original question. This concept of reality influences what is thought to be worth knowing and the process through which it is discovered. For example, questions are likely to be asked that can be answered with quantitative data.

In naturalistic inquiry, multiple realities are acknowledged. Realities are believed to be constructed by individuals. That is, reality does not exist "out there," but in the minds of people and, consequently, is different for each individual (Guba & Lincoln,

Table 5
Logical Positivism and Naturalistic Inquiry Assumptions

Conventional	Emergent
Assumptions	
Single, objective reality can be known, predicted, and controlled.	Multiple realities are constructed, determined individually.
Objective investigator, independent of that which is observed.	Observer is part of what is being studied, inextricably intertwined with that which is observed.
Knowledge is nomothetic, law-based; research results are generalizable.	Knowledge is idiographic, context-bound; research results not generalizable.
Existence of linear cause-effect relationships in a world of determinacy, mechanism, and assembly.	Single cause-effect relationships do not exist; intricate, complex mutual shaping events characterize interactions in an ever-evolving ecology.
Research Design	
Design is developed a priori with detailed specifications re: population, research questions-hypotheses, and research techniques/instrumentation.	Inquiry design is a plan for certain broad contingencies without exact stipulations; given in advance; emergent, unfolding throughout the research process.
Data Collection	
Surveys, questionnaires, attitude scales, pre- and posttest.	Interviews, persistent observation, document analysis.
Data Analysis	
Deductive process, statistical testing and compilation.	Inductive process, develop categories of data—constant comparison method, delimit theory.

1985). (By now these propositions should sound familiar; they were introduced in chapter 1 and have surfaced repeatedly).

The second axiom is epistemological; that is, what is the relationship of the investigator to that which is studied? Logical positivism assumes that the observer or investigator is independent of whatever is being observed; if appropriate inquiry techniques are used, neither the observer nor that which is observed will be influenced by the observation process (including experimental or data collection activities such as an interview or pencil and paper survey questionnaire). Also, an objective inquiry process implies that an investigator's own values and preferences affect neither what is observed nor the meaning given to the observation.

In contrast, Heisenberg (chapter 1) and those committed to the emergent paradigm acknowledge that an observer or investigator is unavoidably part of what is being studied; that which is observed and the observer are inextricably intertwined. The values of the investigator and participant-respondents are also always at work, influencing the problem selected for study, how the problem is defined, and the interpretations given to the findings. Simply put, naturalistic inquiry recognizes that an investigator can never be independent of what is being studied.

The third axiom deals with the concept of generalizability. Logical positivism assumes that the purpose of research is to predict when, where, for whom, and under what conditions laws and principles of behavior will apply. That is, "truth" can be discovered that can be applied to other problems or behaviors regardless of time or context. Sometimes, caveats about the limitations of the generalizability of the findings are appended.

Within the naturalistic inquiry paradigm, knowledge is idiographic (particular to the context) and cannot be generalized to other settings or persons, no matter how similar the settings or participants seem to be. Life—the subject of inquiry—is complex; behavior in the "real" world is idiosyncratic, unique to its context, and difficult (impossible) to predict.

The role of causation is the subject of the fourth axiom. Positivists assume linear cause-effect relationships (recall *post hoc ergo propter hoc* from chapter 2). Naturalism assumes that single cause-effect relationships do not exist. Human experience is more accurately represented by complex, mutually shaping events and actions occurring within multiple open systems suspended in an ever-evolving ecology. Profiles of students' biographical characteristics and behavior, even those that employ sophisticated statistical controls (i.e., variables are manipulated so that differences in results are not mistakenly attributed to variables not of interest to the investigator) cannot adequately represent the complexity and depth of the human experience.

A TRUNCATED OVERVIEW OF NATURALISTIC INQUIRY

In this section we provide a brief overview of the naturalistic inquiry process.[2] It is tempting to draw comparisons with counterpart methods from the familiar conventional paradigm, grounded in logical positivism. However, because conventional inquiry methods are so pervasive in our journals and in our classrooms, we have elected to allow the reader to imagine such comparisons when necessary. After outlining the process, we provide a couple of examples of how naturalistic inquiry might be used in student affairs.

Naturalistic inquiry is interactive, synergistic, emergent inquiry that takes place in situ; that is, the natural setting of whatever is to be studied (Lincoln & Guba, 1985). A naturalistic research design or plan of study is emergent in that decisions about problem definitions and data collection (from whom, when, how) are not made a priori. Rather, these decisions are made as the investigator becomes more knowledgeable about the phenomenon under study. As the investigator becomes intimately acquainted with the problems or activities inherent in a setting, the boundaries or parameters of the study become more obvious and give direction to the study.

Purposive sampling techniques are preferred over other forms of selecting participants. The sample is selected as the study unfolds in order to ensure that information is obtained from those with important, useful perspectives on the issue or problem being examined. Random sampling is viewed as undesirable because someone with something useful to say may be excluded. Patton (1980) provides a detailed discussion of purposive sampling techniques.

When the phenomena to be studied are complex human and organizational interactions not readily translatable into numbers, qualitative data collection methods are preferred (Lincoln & Guba, 1985). Qualitative methods include observations, unobtrusive measures, interviews, and document or record analyses. Although most studies reported in student affairs journals rely on pencil and paper instruments (Kuh et al., 1986a), the data collection instrument of choice in naturalistic inquiry is the investigator. Only the human instrument can use intuition and tacit knowledge as well as reason and logic in collecting and analyzing information. And only the human instrument can accumulate understanding with sensitivity to context, to the perceptual world of respondents, and to the investigator's own beliefs, values, and assumptions. The role of the inquirer and the relationship of the inquirer to the setting and to the information that is collected must be negotiated early in the inquiry process and renegotiated as the study evolves.

The use of qualitative methods (see Miles & Huberman, 1984; Yin, 1984) requires that analysis of data occur throughout a study (during an interview, after first-round interviews have been completed, during and after pertinent documents have been read). This is in stark contrast to many conventional paradigm research studies in which data are not analyzed until after all data have been collected.

The naturalistic inquirer works inductively as the need to prove or disprove theory determined a priori is irrelevant. Theory in the naturalistic setting must be "grounded"; that is, "theory that follows from the data" (Lincoln & Guba, 1985, p. 204). A priori theory cannot anticipate all the information and issues that a researcher using naturalistic methods will encounter, nor can it be expected to explain all the data that are gathered. In addition, a predetermined theoretical framework is likely to unduly restrict the kind of information sought and obtained by the researcher, obscuring some things, illuminating others (Charmaz, 1983).

Grounded theory also requires that data analysis be continuous, and occur at the same time as data collection. Theory is constructed from the researcher's interpretation of data, which is developed in the process of identifying patterns, relationships, and meanings. Thus, grounded theory, like the rest of the naturalistic inquiry process, is emergent—an evolutionary and never-ending expansion and refinement of understanding of the behavior or event under study (Lincoln & Guba, 1985).

This is not to suggest that someone using naturalistic methods rejects or disapproves of extant theory. To the extent possible, theory is used to frame open-ended questions that ensure that participant-respondents have considered factors or issues found to be important in other studies.

The findings of a naturalistic study can be reported in various formats. Stories, trials, and theatrical performances may be appropriate vehicles through which to communicate the results, depending on the audience and the nature of the information to be reported. But in most instances, a "thick" (full of illustrations, detail, and anecdotes) written case report will suffice. Because of the nature of the study and the problems examined, the report must emphasize idiographic (the particulars of the case) dimensions; generalizations are not warranted and cannot be sustained.

Procedures have been standardized to estimate the validity and reliability of conventional paradigm inquiry methods. Guidelines have also been developed whereby the trustworthiness of findings produced using naturalistic methods can be estimated. According to Guba (1981), four criteria should be applied:

1. Credibility (in place of internal validity) addresses the truth value of the inquiry. Lincoln and Guba (1985) strongly advise that interpretations and conclusions be negotiated with those who must live with the results (if an evaluation report or policy analysis), or those purportedly described or analyzed in the study (if a research or case study report).

2. Transferability (in place of external validity) refers to the basic question of applicability of the findings in other contexts. The question of transferability cannot be answered by the investigator, but only by the person seeking to apply the findings.

3. Dependability (in place of reliability) responds to the question of acceptability of the inquiry process. In order to ensure dependability, some method of categorizing data must

be devised. One popular technique is the constant comparative method (Glaser & Strauss, 1967; see also Lincoln & Guba, 1985).

4. Confirmability (in place of objectivity) ensures that the findings and interpretations are supported by the data and are internally consistent. An audit trail, not unlike that used by an accountant, is maintained so that tentative conclusions can be traced back to supporting documentation (Skrtic, 1985).

This abbreviated review of naturalistic inquiry does not do justice to the elegant formulations put forth by its proponents (Guba, 1981; Lincoln & Guba, 1985). Nevertheless, we hope the correspondence between emergent paradigm qualities and naturalistic inquiry axioms and methods are more clear. Two illustrations of what naturalistic inquiry techniques look like in the student affairs context follow.

Examining Student Development Theory in Practice

Proponents of student development have long argued that human development theory should be used to guide the behavior of student affairs staff when working with students. But, as is the case with most knowledge application questions, relatively little is known about what the use of student development theory in the practice of student affairs work looks like. Questionnaire surveys (Strange & Contomanolis, 1983) and analysis of workshop presentations (Kuh, Dannells, Doherty, & Ganshaw, 1977) provide some information about espoused theory in use, but such methods cannot capture the complexities of the work environment and the diversity of the students and faculty groups with which student affairs staff must contend.

What if naturalistic inquiry methods were used to answer the question, "What does the concept of student development look like when it is used in student affairs practice?" One is likely to start where most inquiries begin: finding out what is known about the general problem. After reviewing the literature and deciding on a conceptual framework[3] to guide the inquiry—one that is compatible with the axioms of naturalistic inquiry—one or more institutions must be selected that have a reputation for at least espousing the importance of student development in doing student affairs work. Because naturalistic studies are labor-intensive, and because no conventional claims to generalizability can be made, selecting one institution for thorough study would be acceptable, if not preferable.

After obtaining permission to examine the institution, the researcher must negotiate with the chief student affairs officer (CSAO) and others the terms and parameters of the research activities within and around the division of student affairs. Although the investigator may have some idea of where, from whom, and how pertinent information can be obtained (e.g., analysis of division goal statements and annual reports; interviews with CSAO and staff from all or selected student affairs departments, observations of student-staff interactions), such ideas remain tentative and open to revision until the investigator arrives on the campus and becomes more familiar with the setting, personnel, and aims of the division. For example, interviews with an initial set of participants may lead the investigator to other individuals or documentation not considered at the outset of the study.

To conduct productive interviews and document analysis, the investigator must rely on the literature describing extant knowledge in use (Argyris & Schon, 1978), implementation theory, and student development, and tacit knowledge of the problems encountered in trying to apply theory to practice. The investigator must also develop rapport with participants and estimate the degree to which his or her presence may influence what staff do. The investigator's interactions will also affect interpretations of what is observed (mutual shaping). Other questions asked by the investigator might include: How does the institutional context influence the behavior of staff, and the implementation of student development concepts? Is the president vocally supportive of student affairs and student development goals as articulated by the student affairs division? Are faculty knowledgeable about and interested in what student affairs staff do with students? What do students say about the role of student affairs staff and the quality of the students' experiences during college? These are rather general, starting point questions. As the investigator interacts with participant-respondents, the flow of conversation combined with tacit knowledge and extant theory will generate person- and problem-specific queries.

Whatever the investigator discovers about how, when, and to what extent the student development concept is used by student affairs staff, these findings must be interpreted within the institutional context in which the study was conducted. For example, any social and political influences must be acknowledged (if the CSAO is about to take a new job, staff may say or do unusual or different things).

The investigator's interpretations must also be shared and negotiated with the participant-respondents. Are the investigator's impressions of staff activities consistent with what the staff believe they are doing? The report should, to the greatest extent possible, reflect the world through the eyes of the respondents. Because differences in perceptions are likely to exist, inherently contradictory material may be included. If great differences in perceptions are encountered, they may be explained or accommodated in a minority report.

A naturalistic study of the constructions of student development in a division of student affairs can be quite revealing. The complexity and multiple challenges facing student affairs work will probably be recorded as important, mediating contextual variables. An important outcome of this research technique will be what participant-respondents learn about their work—throughout the process—as a result of talking about what they do.[4]

Estimating the Quality of Student Life

Understanding students' behavior requires the capacity to use multiple perspectives (Kuh, 1984a) to produce multiple meanings and to become actively engaged in the campus community. To know what students are about, student affairs staff must be involved with students in living environments, the library, the athletic field, the union, and other places frequented by students. We must take great care that we are not systematically blinded by our own biases (Kuh, 1981b, 1984b; Schwartz & Ogilvy, 1979) or limited by the narrow range of responses typically available on pencil and paper instruments.

Hermeneutics, the science or art of interpretation (Reason & Rowan, 1981), has been used by literary critics to distill deeper, richer understandings from written works (Campbell, 1986). For example, a biblical scholar, using the principles of hermeneutics, would not develop a priori case study protocols to collect information about a book or chapter from the Bible. Rather, the scholar first reads through all the material (a book, chapter, or perhaps even the entire Bible!) to gain a sense of the general contents, the stories, and the writers' perspectives. After becoming oriented to the entire work, the scholar then painstakingly goes through each of the verses, chapters, and books and carefully records his or her reactions to, and understandings of, the material. This is done until all the material is covered. Then the scholar is in a position to compare specifics from each of the verses, chapters, or books within the general context of the entire work. But the scholar is not yet satisfied; the analysis is not complete. With a better understanding of the respective contributions of the chapters or books of the Bible, the scholar would proceed to read the entire work again. Through several iterations, moving from the general to the specific and back, the scholar uses the information gained from specific scrutiny to capture a more informed sense of the contributions of the entire work. Thus, the hermeneutic process uncovers deeper, richer, more complicated relationships between the various parts of the whole (E. Guba, personal communication, August 1985).

A variant of hermeneutics could be used to estimate the shared reality of students living in a specific residence hall or fraternity house. A student affairs staff member might use a hermeneutic circle to create more elaborate, and perhaps more representative, understandings of what groups of students feel and think about their experiences. Each student is assumed to have information about the experience of all students (the emergent paradigm quality of holonomy). One student is interviewed to get a general sense of the concerns and issues important to that student. The staff member then moves to a second student, encouraging him or her to identify important concerns or issues. After the second student has exhausted his or her own concerns, the interviewer may mention issues presented by the first student but not mentioned by the second student, and encourage the second student to comment on those issues, if the student is willing. By using this process to interview a group of students, a more comprehensive understanding about issues and concerns can be gleaned while ameliorating the pernicious influence of one interviewer's biases or the interests of a narrowly circumscribed group of students (E. Guba, personal communication, August 1985).

A MODEST INQUIRY AGENDA

As grist for the emergent paradigm inquiry mill, we present our "top 10," the issues that most need to be addressed by student affairs knowledge producers. In our opinion, all of these problems could be examined using naturalistic methods. We have categorized the problems under three distinct forms of knowledge production (research, evaluation, and policy analysis) as defined by Lincoln and Guba (1985).

Research

Research is disciplined inquiry conducted to analyze a problem in order to achieve understanding or to facilitate action (Lincoln & Guba, 1985). Research is not necessarily intended for use in decision making or determining program efficacy, although it is sometimes used in that manner.

1. What are the contributions that student affairs makes to the quality of campus life? This question has begged for a data-based answer for a long, long time. Canons of logical positivism have precluded accepting students' reports about the meaning of the college experience in general. Compared with conventional forms of inquiry, naturalistic inquiry methods are more appropriate for responding to this type of broad question that touches all segments of a student affairs division and requires input from faculty, students, and others.

2. What is the relationship between participation in extracurricular activities and college outcomes? We have a few studies that link leadership experiences with success after college (e.g., Schuh & Laverty, 1983), but we really understand very little about what students think the benefits are of participation and to what those benefits are related during and after college.

3. What is the influence of peers on students' achievement, attitudes, motivation, and personality development during college? Given the large amount of college outcomes literature, it may seem surprising that this question makes our top 10. For example, although numerous studies have been made of roommate compatibility, we know relatively little about the mutual shaping that occurs in such relationships, and even less about the influence of a wider circle of peers (Astin, 1985). Not since Leemon (1972) has there been an ethnographic portrayal of the ways in which a living unit (e.g., a fraternity) exerts influence over its members; in fact, studies of the fraternity and sorority experience are noteworthy by their absence from the student affairs literature during the past 18 years (Kuh et al., 1986a).

4. What is going to college like? (How's that for a fuzzy problem statement?) This question could take the naturalistic inquirer in a number of directions. For example, what does the minority student or adult learner experience look like from a self-organizing, developmental perspective (Caple, 1985; 1987)? Adopting the dissipative structures framework (Sawada & Caley, 1985), how does the developmental process unfold for the traditional age college student?[5]

5. Are the conventional paradigm concepts of challenge and support valid in the framework of self-organization theory? If not, what concepts and behaviors might take their place? As we discussed earlier, the emergent paradigm will force us to rethink our understanding of the developmental process. Naturalistic inquiry may be useful in increasing our understanding of the dissipative, self-reordering nature of growth during the college years because it allows the researcher to focus on issues that students and the researcher consider important as the study unfolds. That is, the

researcher is not constrained by a priori questions that may not be related to first- and second-order developmental changes.

Evaluation

Evaluation is inquiry undertaken to determine the merit or worth of a program or individual performance level for the purposes of improvement or refinement (formative evaluation) or estimation of impact (summative evaluation) (Lincoln & Guba, 1985). Note that the purpose of evaluation is to estimate the value of the activity whereas research makes no value claim.

6. What is the value of learning skills programs and other activities designed to upgrade the academic skills of underprepared college students? Although many more students from educationally disadvantaged backgrounds have entered colleges and universities during the past decade (Hodgkinson, 1985), relatively few studies of learning skills programs have been reported in the literature (Kuh et al., 1986a). Those that have appeared tend to focus on easily measured or quantifiable matters such as semester grades and persistence rates. Quality of life side effects, such as the importance of learning to live in a pluralistic society, are rarely addressed.

7. Are student activities worth the cost? This type of question is scary; it gets right to the heart of our work. We know little about cost-benefit relationships in student affairs. In part, this is because it is extremely difficult to accurately estimate either the costs associated with a program or set of functions or the benefits of participation in the program (Kuh & Nuss, in press). On the surface, cost-benefit analyses call for a linear, quantitative model consistent with conventional inquiry approaches. But costs and benefits mean different things to different people in different contexts. Interviews with parents, trustees, and legislators may provide useful information when weighing the importance of extracurricular activities against other programs competing for the same funds.

Policy Analysis

Policy analysis is inquiry designed to gather and display evidence for and against alternative policy options to ensure that the values of relevant audiences are considered in deliberations (Lincoln & Guba, 1985). Very few policy analysis articles appear in student affairs journals; indeed, the number of such articles published in the past 18 years has declined for unknown reasons (Kuh et al., 1986a). However, the need to know how student life policies are developed and what impact they have has never been greater.

8. How are student life policies formulated and implemented? Our experience is that most student affairs staff members are not knowledgeable about the process of policy development. Despite their responsibilities for implementation of student life policy, staff often overlook the amount of discretion (and therefore influence) they exert in determining the meaning of policy in their setting (Lipsky, 1980). At the least, "thick" descriptions of student life policy formulation would make for interesting reading, and would provide a useful framework within which to interpret information gathered to address the next policy question.

9. What is the relationship between student life policy and student development? We know of no studies that have examined the influence of policy as intended, as implemented, or as experienced on students' development.[6] Intended policy effects can be relatively easily determined from an analysis of policy documents and discussions with campus administrators. The possible influence of various policy options as implemented by staff at various levels and as experienced by students is more difficult to estimate but would be of great value in formulating and revising campus policies.

10. What student life policy options are compatible with the values and life styles of minority cultures? Some literature on the minority student experience in higher education suggests that the campus culture is often perceived by minority students as inhospitable (Astin, 1982). To what extent do student life policies exacerbate or alleviate this perception? What policy options can be generated to enhance the quality of life of minority students?

Toward More Interesting Writing (and Reading!)

There is no guarantee that if a greater number of researchers in student affairs or allied fields embraces the emergent paradigm and publishes studies using qualitative methods, what is published in student affairs journals will immediately be of greater interest and use to practitioners. Much depends on the creativity and insightfulness of those conducting the inquiry.

We believe that inquiry methods compatible with the emergent paradigm have the potential to influence in a positive manner the classical professional writing style—dry, explanatory rhetoric written in the third person. Only a few years ago, magisterial style writers, such as Kenneth Boulding, would have lacked credibility in many circles (Leontief, 1986). Perhaps it's time that the concise, reserved, and usually colorless language that dominates articles in most higher education and student affairs journals be replaced by more persuasive communication that appeals to a greater range of emotions as well as the intellect and more accurately reflects the ambiguity and complexity of student affairs work. Perhaps more frequent use of metaphors and puns (e.g., "an ecosystem that becomes an echosystem," Boulding, 1985) will enliven discourse in our publications and encourage the introduction of new terms that more effectively capture the dynamic nature of student development and administrative challenges characteristic of IHEs.

SUMMARY

The conventional approach to knowledge production, supported by the axioms of logical positivism, is not likely to be sustained through this century. This is not to say that the revolution will happen overnight. The positivist bias will continue to operate, and articles using qualitative techniques grounded in naturalistic inquiry will meet with resistance for some time. But sooner or later (by now you know we prefer the former!) the necessary critical mass of knowledge producers and gatekeepers will recognize and accept New Story, naturalistic ways of knowing as legitimate. Such methods are not only an attractive alternative, but are absolutely necessary to describe and make meaning of the complex and mutual shaping interactions that occur within the campus milieu.

Faculty and student life researchers are encouraged to experiment with naturalistic inquiry methods in studying college students. The student affairs field has certain traditions that are quite compatible with these methods. For example, an appreciation, indeed a reverence, for becoming engaged—both intellectually and emotionally—in students' development and individual and group decision-making processes characterizes our field. The act of engagement surely influences what students and student affairs staff experience and how they experience it. Engagement should also characterize the inquiry process in student affairs work.

NOTES

1. "Dust-bowl empiricism" referred to the pervasive preference for the quantitative, number-crunching, positivist approach to behavioral and social science research for which preparation programs at several Midwestern universities (Iowa, Minnesota, Missouri) and the University of Maryland were noted.
2. Lincoln and Guba (1985) and others have written volumes attempting to explicate appropriate methods for conducting naturalistic inquiry. We do not encourage someone unfamiliar with naturalistic methods to conduct a study based on this description alone. If you find the description provocative and inviting, consult *Naturalistic Inquiry* (Lincoln & Guba, 1985) or some other text that treats the topic in considerable and necessary depth.
3. We did not purposefully understate the amount of time and effort typically required to develop a framework within which such a study can be concep-

tualized . . . but it is badly understated. Creating an appropriate framework may take almost as much time as collecting the data.

4. We are always amazed at the response to the question, "What is it that you do?" The initial response is a paraphrase of the job title. Our next question is, "Well, tell us something about what you do on your job?" This usually results in less than 30 seconds of awkward phrases. We persist until the respondent starts to become familiar with the answer and begins to talk in somewhat more detail about what he or she does. Invariably the initial period of awkwardness is explained by two factors: (a) nobody asked that question before—meaning no one really wanted to know what I do; or (b) I had trouble talking about what I do because I had not stopped to think about it before!

5. Several excellent case studies of the experiences of individual students were published in the 1950s and 1960s (Madison, 1969; White, 1966); of course, they were grounded and interpreted in conventional paradigm assumptions about growth and development.

6. Guba (1985) distinguished between policy as intended by policymakers, policy as implemented by those responsible for implementation (residence hall staff), and policy as experienced by those for whom the policy was developed (students). These distinctions have particular heuristic power for understanding the influence of student life policy on student behavior.

CHAPTER 7

IMPLICATIONS FOR STUDENT AFFAIRS PREPARATION PROGRAMS

> *For every time she shouted, "Fire,"*
> *They only answered "Little Liar!"*
> *And therefore when her Aunt returned*
> *Matilda, and the House, were burned.*
>
> —Hilaire Belloc

> *Of course we all have our limits, but how can you possibly find your*
> *boundaries unless you explore as far and wide as you possibly can? I would*
> *rather fail in an attempt at something new and uncharted than safely succeed*
> *in a repeat of something I have done.*
>
> —A. E. Hotchner

The paradigmatic odyssey cannot be completed without considering implications of the emergent paradigm for student affairs preparation programs. In this chapter, some of the general problems likely to be encountered in incorporating radical material—such as that embodied by the emergent paradigm—in traditional preparation programs are discussed. We conclude with an analysis of what must occur if student affairs preparation programs are to accommodate emergent paradigm concepts in the preparation of student affairs practitioners and scholars.

READY OR NOT, HERE IT COMES!

As in other human services (e.g., social work, school counseling), the number of student affairs preparation programs increased during the 1960s. Periodicals specific to various aspects of student affairs work were created to share developments and research findings (Kuh, Bean, Bradley, Coomes, & Hunter, 1986). Gradually, student services and preparation programs evolved toward greater standardization. Various groups (e.g., American College Personnel Association, National Association of Student Personnel Administrators) attempted to regulate access to the field by establishing standards for accreditation of preparation programs and campus services. By the mid-1980s, what was once a loose federation of practitioners from diverse backgrounds joined together by an altruistic interest in the welfare of college students had evolved into a guild-like society with specialized functions grounded in human development and organizational theory, entry qualifications, and differentiated standards.

Graduate courses in student affairs are currently grounded in the behavioral and social sciences (Rodgers, 1977). Preparation programs give student affairs work credibility and provide an environment in which issues in the field can be addressed and knowledge can be produced. Future student affairs staff are thereby introduced to the philosophy and rich traditions of the field. That's the good news.

The bad news is that student affairs preparation programs are firmly entrenched in conventional paradigm assumptions (see Table 6). Evidence of these assumptions can be found in the movement to develop standards for preparation programs and in increasingly specialized curricula.

Table 6
Implications of Conventional and Emergent Paradigm Assumptions for Student Affairs Preparation Programs

Conventional	Emergent
Curriculum grounded in social and behavioral science research.	Self-organizing curriculum open to shaping by students and faculty through shared experiences and informed by diverse disciplinary perspectives.
Accreditation standards used to ensure quality preparation.	Implicit and explicit expectations for preparation programs open to challenge and morphogenetic change; context determines content and process.
Curriculum advocates linear causality, determinacy, objective reality, and positivistic inquiry methods.	Curriculum advocates holonomy, multiple realities, indeterminacy, and complicated perspectival sense-making to challenge conventional assumptions.
Research grounded in positivist assumptions and methods and conducted by detached, objective inquirer.	Research grounded in naturalism and conducted by inquirer seeking holistic and context-informed understanding using qualitative methods.
Curriculum tends to be prescriptive and time-bound.	Open-ended, flexible expectations for length and content of graduate study.
Hierarchical learning arrangements (faculty make curriculum decisions and teach and mentor students).	Heterarchical learning opportunities (faculty learn from as well as teach students and vice versa) are purposefully arranged.

The current accreditation effort in student affairs (Council for the Advancement of Standards, 1986) may be useful for some purposes. Reasonable standards rigorously monitored may lead to improvements in the form and substance of preparation program curricula. It is possible that the existence of standards may enhance the quality of some programs; those programs that do not meet the standards may seem less attractive to some prospective students.

Our concern is that accreditation standards for student affairs preparation programs will do what standards for other fields have done, that is, reinforce the status quo. Kuhn (1970) warned that professionalization of a field tends to reduce receptivity to challenges to standard practices. Accreditation movements in particular are likely to have a chilling effect on innovations and ideas that contradict extant beliefs and practices. To the extent that this is—or will be—characteristic of the effect of accreditation on student affairs, curricular modifications congenial with the emergent paradigm may encounter numerous obstacles.

Over the past two decades, specialization of functions has characterized the field as roles such as career planning specialists, financial need analysts, and student development specialists have become more common. We are not advocating that student affairs staff avoid acquiring technical information and expertise to perform certain necessary functions such as interpretation of a vocational interest inventory or federal financial aid policies.

Within the New Story, however, there will be a greater demand for flexible, responsive generalists, not specialists. Therefore, preparation program faculty must do what they can to encourage students to acquire a broad understanding of, and experience with, the full range of functions performed by student affairs and the ways in which these functions complement the institution's mission. Diversity in students and in institutional forms must also be addressed during graduate study as society and societal institutions evolve toward greater pluralism (see Table 6).

A bold effort on the part of faculty and practitioners will be required to use knowledge from other fields to inform student affairs practice. A renewed sense of experimentation and innovation will be needed to become familiar with ways of knowing compatible with the emergent paradigm. Conventional theories of human development must be reconceptualized, and the concepts of morphogenesis, mutual shaping, multiple realities, indeterminacy, and holonomy must be acknowledged, and incorporated in courses and consultations whenever possible. Most student affairs preparation programs do little to acknowledge the importance of holonomy and mutual shaping. The typical student affairs master's degree program is composed of discrete courses that may or may not build on or reinforce one another. Integrating experiences tend to be few and far between, and faculty rarely participate in colleagues' classes to assess and to demonstrate the interconnectedness of the curriculum. As a result, courses are linked only on a program outline sheet, not by cumulative knowledge and shared understandings.

With evidence of the emergent paradigm everywhere and with educational reform a national mandate, now is a propitious time for innovative curriculum reform in student affairs. Although much can be learned from earlier curriculum reform efforts (Arner, Peterson, Arner, Hawkins, & Spooner, 1976; Knock, 1977; Rentz, 1976; Spooner, 1979),[1] we must not allow our imagination to be constrained by previous conventional paradigm approaches to the preparation of student affairs staff. Let us be more specific about what will be required to support experimentation with emergent paradigm concepts in preparation programs (see Table 6).

CHARACTERISTICS OF EMERGENT PARADIGM PREPARATION PROGRAMS

At the beginning of chapter 3, we briefly described the anomie and doubt physicists, such as Einstein and Heisenberg, experienced when they encountered concepts that did not make sense within the laws and norms of conventional physics. Confronted with what may be described as an existential crisis, Einstein, Heisenberg, and their colleagues felt lost and bewildered for a time. We don't wish to overstate this, but more than a few preparation program faculty and graduate students may find themselves in a similar plight when confronted with the implications of the emergent paradigm for student affairs preparation and practice.

Although most student affairs graduate programs are administratively assigned to schools, colleges, and departments of education, they are distinct from other fields of study within education. Graduates of our programs do not seek jobs in public schools and, therefore, our curriculum is not bound by state education department requirements. This situation has advantages and disadvantages. On the one hand faculty have almost complete curricular autonomy (or did until the development of the CAS Standards). On the other hand, few faculty outside of the student affairs preparation program have more than a foggy notion of what goes on in our programs and what kinds of jobs our graduates obtain.[2] As a consequence, preparation program requirements must be credible in as many areas as possible (e.g, traditional admissions criteria, such as high undergraduate grade point average and Graduate Record Examination scores, required statistics and research design courses, etc.). The rejection of conventional beliefs can be threatening in an environment, such as graduate school, that tends to be epistemologically conservative. That is, professional preparation programs in general are not known for innovation and risk-taking in the methods used to examine practices and knowledge in the field.[3] Faculty of student affairs preparation programs in particular may feel constrained to organize the content and structure of graduate study in a manner that has become traditionally credible. Thus, for both epistemological and reputational reasons, warmly embracing the emergent paradigm will not be easy. But for those willing to try, we offer some suggestions.[4]

Instruction

Student affairs preparation programs must become more multi- and transdisciplinary (Reinharz, 1981). For many years, student affairs preparation programs at the master's level were criticized for simply being a hodgepodge of courses from different departments glued together by an introductory course and a practicum (Knock, 1977). We are not suggesting a return to the good old days! But we do recommend at least one course that treats ways of knowing from historical and social science perspectives that would address the emergent paradigm, in addition to at least one statistics or conventional paradigm research design course.[5] In addition, ways of knowing practiced in other disciplines such as the humanities and natural sciences will be extremely useful to student affairs staff experiencing the paradigm shift.

We do not believe it is reasonable to expect master's level candidates to independently conduct conventional or naturalistic studies after only one research course. We do believe it is desirable, if not essential, however, that they be aware of the shift in paradigms and recognize conventional and emergent assumptions when they are encountered in practice.

Doctoral students are advised to take courses in history and philosophy of social science that introduce concepts and vocabularies that enable them to conduct and critique research and administrative practice in both conventional and emergent paradigm language. At this level, students must have two or more conventional inquiry courses so that they are not viewed and dismissed as interlopers or misinformed outsiders who do not have the expertise to conduct research within or render informed judgments about the conventional paradigm. Grounding in conventional inquiry also gives students a basis for comparison with emergent methods so that inquiry techniques appropriate to a particular problem or context can be selected (Reinharz, 1981).

In addition, at least one (preferably more) course that addresses emergent paradigm research methodology and methods (naturalistic inquiry, ethnographic methods, qualitative inquiry techniques) is essential. For those with interests in knowledge production, internship or practicum experiences in naturalistic inquiry will also be very useful.

If coursework in epistemology, conventional and emergent research methods, and social science can be obtained from faculty outside the preparation program, so much the better. By taking courses outside of the program major, students can examine the applicability of challenges to conventional concepts and principles within other disciplines to the practice of student affairs and higher education administration.

In the current CAS standards (1986), three types of approved preparation programs are described: counseling, student development, and administration. The conceptual framework for these program tracks was based on the results of a study of preparation program curricula conducted in the mid-1970s (Rodgers, 1977). Although the specific courses in each CAS program track have been modified several times since then, we do not believe that emergent paradigm principles are adequately reflected in the standards. For example, although naturalistic research methods are mentioned as an option in the organizational behavior and development component of the student development and administration tracks, naturalistic inquiry is not specifically addressed in the research and evaluation component. Although it could be argued that the description of research and evaluation (CAS, 1986, p. 105) is general enough to include any inquiry paradigm, it is not likely that naturalistic inquiry will be emphasized given the disjunct between conventional, positivist assumptions and emergent paradigm assumptions.

Students are also required, by CAS standards, to have at least one practical experience "with a project designed to *facilitate* [italics added] human development" (CAS, 1986, p. 107). As we asserted in chapter 3, intentional efforts to systematically influence human behavior are incompatible with the emergent paradigm.

We strongly encourage those charged with interpreting and applying the standards to be flexible in their reviews of programs that are attempting to integrate emergent paradigm learnings through alternative coursework. For example, it may be that to acquaint students with both conventional and naturalistic methodology, a history and philosophy of social science course must be substituted for a traditional required course, such as counseling, or even a practicum.

Of course, it is unlikely that students will elect such a course without considerable support and encouragement from the faculty. Acknowledgment of the importance of the emergent paradigm by the core faculty is critical if the field is to manage the transition from a conventional to an emergent set of assumptions and beliefs about student development and the organization and administration of IHEs. We will return to this point shortly.

Skill Training

The emergent paradigm calls us to help others discover and make meaning of their experiences and, further, to respectfully acknowledge and celebrate experiences that are different from our own. The student affairs staff member of the future must be prepared to engage in "reciprocal encounters" (Reinharz, 1981)—to listen and to share information, insight, and power with colleagues and students. Through the process of sharing our own interpretations and desires, we mutually shape the environment in ways that can have an empowering influence on students, faculty, and others.

To the extent possible, student affairs staff must acquire—if they have not already done so—an appreciation for different forms of oral and written communication. As we mentioned in the preceding chapter, the dry, unimaginative prose common to conventional science usually does not capture the full range of human experience, particularly in the affective domain. In an attempt to describe the depth and richness of the human experience, the language of the poet has evolved differently from that of the social scientist. Developing a clear, but flexible dialectical writing style that embraces one or more of these "languages" will be even more important than it is at present as we acknowledge pluralism, mutual shaping, and the interconnectedness between the intellectual and affective domains.[6]

It will be important for doctoral students and many master's degree candidates to acquire or hone qualitative data collection skills, including observation, interview (both open-ended and unstructured), group facilitation skills, and persuasive, entrepreneurial behavior useful for encouraging students and colleagues to participate in the double looping or action learning activities described in chapter 5.

Perhaps the most important area of skill training is in the area that student affairs staff claim as their greatest contribution: personal development. We often understate the importance of a staff member's personal development during graduate study. But the emergent paradigm, with its emphasis on multiple realities, the indeterminate nature of individual and organizational behavior, and heterarchical interactions will be especially advantageous to persons who are self-directed, introspective, and assertive, and who can comfortably interact with, and appreciate the differences between and among a wide range of people. Fortunately, many student affairs workers exhibit such traits.

In addition, to manage the transition to the emergent paradigm, student affairs staff must examine comfortable ways of defining reality and become cognizant of biases and preferences that influence their interactions with others. The process of self-discovery, long an espoused student development goal, must be re-emphasized within student affairs preparation programs so that student affairs workers are comfortable in dealing with issues that conflict with personal values and beliefs and in confronting ambiguity, diversity, and deviance (Reinharz, 1981) (see Figure 10).

FIGURE 10
Reciprocal Encounters

Source: Drawing by Matt Groening from *Love Is Hell*; copyright 1986, Pantheon Books, a division of Random House, Inc.

Resources

The most precious resources in any preparation program are students and faculty. The demographics of the professoriate suggest that well over half of those persons currently in faculty positions will retire between now and the year 2000, assuming a retirement age of 65 (Bowen & Schuster, 1986). If these data accurately describe student affairs faculty,[7] at least two "predictions" can be offered, both of which are plausible. First, we might expect a sizable new cohort of faculty to join student affairs preparation programs in the next two decades. This is likely to have significant implications for innovation and change in preparation programs, including the kind of material presented in core student affairs courses. For example, by 2001, it is conceivable that many of these new faculty will be well grounded in the emergent paradigm.

Trends in faculty demographics also mean, however, that for the forseeable future, preparation programs will be staffed by many faculty currently teaching. Therefore, openness to, and experience with, emergent paradigm principles on the part of present faculty will be essential if the field is to manage the transition from a conventional to an emergent set of assumptions and beliefs about student development and the operation of IHEs.

Compare the description that follows with what you know about people who come through student affairs preparation programs enroute to a job in the field:

> Although some of the skills and self-awareness can be acquired through training, there is a necessary foundation present in some people (and lacking in others) which enables them to operate comfortably in certain cognitive-relational-action modes rather than in others. (Reinharz, 1981, p. 428)

We assume most persons who choose student affairs as a vocation perceive that the field will enable them to capitalize on their strengths. If we can recruit students who have attitudes and behavioral styles that tolerate pluralism, who are willing to take interpersonal risks, and who recognize the value in openly sharing and rigorously examining beliefs, the field will have no trouble accommodating the emergent paradigm.

Some emergent paradigm concepts reflect understandings and interpretations that are so unconventional that it may be impossible to adequately introduce some of these notions in anything less than a 2-year master's degree program. For research oriented programs (PhD), students should be encouraged to take more time than that typically expected in a traditional 3-year residency program. Knowledge producers and scholar-practitioners will need varying amounts of time to process, internalize, and discover applications of emergent paradigm qualities. A time constraint cannot be placed on a process that will demand a considerable amount of creative energy. This will place financial pressure on institutions as more assistantships may be required to support those students selecting the longer time frame.

An adequate amount of physical space should be available so that students can work near one another and, if possible, close to faculty so that comfortable and continuous interaction can occur without demanding extraordinary effort on the part of either students and faculty.[8] Many challenges to comfortable beliefs will be associated with assimilating the emergent paradigm, and a place where students can feel secure and important will ease the process of grappling with these issues.

Students should be encouraged to attend campus colloquia that examine issues related to the emergent paradigm. Often, other departments (psychology, sociology, organizational behavior, and even other education programs!) schedule provocative events that would be quite challenging for the student affairs worker-in-training. As much as possible, preparation programs should also provide students with opportunities to meet with visiting scholars and practitioners of both sexes and of various races and ages who have demonstrated innovative ways of integrating emergent paradigm qualities into their thinking and work (Reinharz, 1981).

Role Models and Peers

A spirit of collaboration between and among faculty and students (i.e., heterarchical behavior) should characterize the program. That is, the primary psychological environment of the program should be supportive, not evaluative (Reinharz, 1981). Folk wisdom suggests that, on the surface at least, many student affairs preparation programs may be congruent with Reinharz's recommendations; we hope so.

Administrators of preparation programs should model and demonstrate a commitment to emergent paradigm principles. Decisions should be shared and derived heterarchically, not through (top down) bureaucratic actions. The program participants should strive for open communication, a sense of esprit de corps and community, and a high level of involvement by students, faculty, and families. Celebration and confirmation of shared experiences through social events such as an annual year-end banquet to bid farewell to graduating students and commemorative academic activities (e.g., qualifying examinations, commencement) are also important.

Finally, faculty should create opportunities to collaborate with students on making presentations and conducting research.

Those with more experience—in teaching, writing, research, supervision of staff and so forth—should be encouraged to work with those with less experience. Chronological age, however, may not be the most important factor in generative behavior. Although faculty can be important role models in many circumstances, students may also be able to serve a generative function (Knefelkamp, 1986). For example, students can help faculty maintain a healthy perspective toward their work by inviting faculty to participate in recreational activities that deemphasize traditional roles of professor and student. Some doctoral students bring rich administrative experience to the classroom and can challenge and support faculty applications of theory to current practice.

SUMMARY

A lot is demanded of student affairs preparation programs. Students are expected to learn substantive content related to the practice of student affairs and acquire research and writing skills. Faculty are expected to produce useful knowledge about the field. Through mutually shaping socialization experiences, students and faculty affirm the importance of student affairs work to IHEs. In the future, student affairs preparation programs must also introduce the emergent paradigm to the field. Although incorporating emergent paradigm qualities in the curriculum won't be impossible, neither will it come easily. Many faculty and students have grown up with and are very comfortable with conventional knowledge production approaches and organizational expectations. Some faculty and more than a few students are likely to experience feelings of dissonance when confronted with the emergent paradigm.

To support experimentation with qualities associated with the emergent paradigm, the preparation program environment must provide ample space (both physical and psychological) and support. The experiences of those grappling to reconcile conventional and emergent ways of making meaning must be publicly confirmed so that all know that the struggle is one that is of importance to the entire community. And all participants in the preparation program must be given responsibility for acquiring expertise in multiple forms of expression and communication. Most important, students must clarify their own assumptions and beliefs about what is personally meaningful or "true." Only by discovering who we are and sharing our discovery with others can we acknowledge that which we cannot know for certain while helping others discover themselves.

NOTES

1. Earlier attempts at curricular reform have been grounded in the conventional paradigm. Familiarity with these efforts provides a sense of perspective on the evolution of the field and should not be routinely dismissed. However, these accounts of curriculum modification underemphasize the energy and patience usually invested. The stamina that will be required to successfully integrate emergent paradigm principles in preparation programs is difficult to over-estimate. We can liken the task to Collins's (1985) description of having an affair with an elephant: It's hard to known where to begin. It will be extremely difficult to reach the objective. Those attempting the feat are likely to get trampled on. And it takes 8 years to get any results.

2. We don't wish to overstate this distinction. Most faculty know only one program well, their own. But there tends to be somewhat more interaction among faculty from various specialities in secondary education (math, social studies, language) and elementary education so that they share a sense of being about the same task: preparing public school teachers. The current interest in reform in teacher education is a good case in point. We doubt that many student affairs preparation program faculty are involved in examination of the teacher education programs on their campus. Through intensive committee work, faculty learn more about other programs; student affairs preparation faculty typically are not involved in those discussions.

3. Some would argue that training programs for professionals in medicine, den-tistry, and law should not be places where a good deal of experimentation is encouraged. Society expects doctors and lawyers to be responsible, highly trained craftspeople who know what works and what does not. When we are scheduled for surgery, most of us would prefer a surgeon who uses well-established tech-niques rather than someone who has developed an appetite for innovation and experimentation.

4. The preparation program elements that require attention were adapted from Reinharz (1981).

5. The instructor for such a course must be chosen very carefully. The bias for the conventional paradigm runs deep, and if the instructor uses the course to critique and dismiss the emergent paradigm, most students would be better off without such an experience.

6. Many students, particularly master's degree students directly from undergrad-uate study, chafe at the writing demands of some courses and are threatened by close critical analyses of their writing. Yet one of the more frequent activities in which student affairs staff must engage is writing—memos, reports, justifi-cations for supplemental budget support, and so on. Typically, former students are very appreciative for the time and energy invested in developing a coherent, articulate writing style.

7. Of the 30 faculty attending the fall, 1986 Midwest Meeting of College Student Personnel Faculty, about one-third expected to retire by 1991; almost half will retire by 1996.

8. Space allocation is always a potentially divisive issue. No matter what policies and priorities are established for space allocation and use, or how those priorities are implemented, few people are elated. We hope you have access to enough space to do some of the things we mentioned.

EPILOGUE

A new age cannot be summoned on request (Lucas, 1984).

"I am going to the Great Oz to ask him to give me some brains," remarked the Scarecrow, "for my head is stuffed with straw."

"And I'm going to ask him to give me a heart," said the Tin Woodman.

"And I'm going to ask him to send Toto and me back to Kansas," added Dorothy.

"Do you think the Wizard could give me courage?" asked the cowardly Lion.

"Just as easily as he could give me brains," said the Scarecrow.

"Then if you don't mind, I'll go with you," said the Lion.

And Dorothy and friends went skipping down the Yellow Brick Road in search of the Wizard.

"You are all wrong," said the little man meekly. "I have been making believe."

"Making believe!" cried Dorothy. "Are you not a great Wizard?"

"Hush my dear," he said. "Don't speak so loud or you will be overheard—and I should be ruined. I'm supposed to be a great Wizard."

"And aren't you?" she asked.

"Not a bit of it, my dear; I'm just a common man."

"You are a very bad man." said Dorothy.

"Oh no, my dear, I'm a very good man; it's just that I'm a very bad Wizard."

Dorothy, the Tin Woodman, and the others had it pretty easy really, when compared with us. Their goal was clear and the path to the goal was clearly marked. All they had to do to find Oz was to follow a yellow brick road. Our journey will be more difficult. The way is not clearly marked, nor will we know if we have met the Great Oz or any other wizards along the way. It's probably just as well, for whatever we discover about students' dreams, fears, and aspirations, whatever we learn about life in institutions of higher education, and whatever we contribute to the quality of student affairs work will be a function of how we choose to interpret the world within an emergent frame of reference.

We can choose to feel lost, like the forest owl from chapter 1 who was unprepared for life in a prairie. Or, we can use our imagination and pretend we are wizards. The choices are ours.

REFERENCES

Allan, L.G., & Jenkins, H.M. (1980). The judgment of contingency and the nature of the response alternatives. *Canadian Journal of Psychology, 34,* 1–11.

American College Personnel Association. (1975). A student development model for student affairs in tomorrow's higher education. *Journal of College Student Personnel, 16,* 334–341.

American Council on Education. (1937, 1949). *The Student personnel point of view.* Washington, DC: American Council on Education.

Appleton, J., Briggs, C., & Rhatigan, J. (1978). *Pieces of eight.* Portland, OR: National Association of Student Personnel Administrators.

Argyris, C., & Schon, D.A. (1978). *Organizational learning: A theory of action perspective.* Reading, MA: Addison-Wesley.

Arner, T.D., Peterson, W.D., Arner, C.A., Hawkins, L.T., & Spooner, S.E. (1976). Student personnel education: A process-outcome model. *Journal of College Student Personnel, 17,* 334–341.

Astin, A.W. (1977). *Four critical years.* San Francisco: Jossey-Bass.

Astin, A.W. (1982). *Minorities in American higher education.* San Francisco: Jossey-Bass.

Astin, A.W. (1985). *Achieving educational excellence.* San Francisco: Jossey-Bass.

Baldridge, J.B., Curtis, D.B., Ecker, G.P., & Riley, G.L. (1977). Alternative models of governance in higher education. In J.B. Baldridge & T. Deal (Eds.), *Governing academic organizations* (pp. 2–25). Berkeley, CA: McCutchan.

Banning, J.H. (Ed.) (1975). *Campus ecology: A perspective for student affairs.* Portland, OR: National Association of Student Personnel Administrators.

Banning, J.H. (1980). The campus ecology manager role. In U. Delworth & G. Hanson (Eds.), *Student services: A handbook for the profession* (pp. 209–227). San Francisco: Jossey-Bass.

Begley, S. (1986, January 20). A fifth force of physics. *Newsweek.*

Berelson, B., & Steiner, G. (1964). *Human behavior: An inventory of findings.* New York: Harcourt, Brace & World.

Bertalanffy, L. von. (1968). *General system theory* (rev. ed.). New York: Braziller.

Bloland, P.A. (1986). Student development: The new orthodoxy? (Part One) *ACPA Developments, 13*(3), 1, 13.

Bohr, N. (1958). *Atomic physics and human knowledge.* New York: Wiley.

Borland, D.T. (1983). Organizational foundations of administration. In T.K. Miller, R.B. Winston, & W.R. Mendenhall (Eds.), *Administration and leadership in student affairs* (pp. 31–51). Muncie, IN: Accelerated Development.

Boulding, K. (1985). *Human betterment.* Beverly Hills, CA: Sage.

Bowen, H.R., & Schuster, J.H. (1986). *American Professors: A national resource imperiled.* New York: Oxford University Press.

Bouwsma, W.J. (1975). The models of the educated man. *American Scholar, 44,* 209.

Bradley, R.K., Coomes, M.D., & Kuh, G.D. (1985). A typology for student affairs knowledge. *Journal of College Student Personnel, 26*, 11–18.

Brown, R.D. (1972). *Tomorrow's higher education: A return to the academy*. Washington, DC: American College Personnel Association.

Cameron, K.S. (1984). Organizational adaptation and higher education. *Journal of Higher Education, 55*, 122–144.

Campbell, C. (1986, February 9). The tyranny of the Yale critics. *New York Times*, pp. 20–26, 28, 43, 47–48.

Campbell, D.T., & Stanley, J.C. (1963). *Experimental and quasi-experimental designs for research*. Chicago: Rand McNally.

Campbell, J. (1982). *Grammatical man: Information, entropy, language, and life*. New York: Simon & Schuster.

Caple, R.B. (1985). Counseling and the self-organization paradigm. *Journal of Counseling and Development, 64*, 173–178.

Caple, R.B. (1987). The change process in developmental theory: A self-organization paradigm, part 1. *Journal of College Student Personnel, 28*, 4–11.

Capra, F. (1976). *The Tao of physics*. Boulder: Shambhala.

Capra, F. (1983). *The turning point: Science, society, and the rising culture*. New York: Basic Books.

Carnegie Foundation for the Advancement of Teaching. (1981). *Common learning: A Carnegie colloquium on general education*. Washington, DC: Carnegie Foundation for the Advancement of Teaching.

Charmaz, K. (1983). The grounded theory method: An explication and interpretation. In R.M. Emerson (Ed.), *Contemporary field research* (pp. 109–126). Boston: Little, Brown.

Chickering, A.W. (1969). *Education and identity*. San Francisco: Jossey-Bass.

Clark, B.R. (1972). Organizational saga in higher education. *Administrative Science Quarterly, 17*, 178–184.

Clark, B.R., Heist, P., McConnell, T.R., Trow, M.A., & Yonge, G. (1972). *Students and colleges: Interaction and change*. Berkeley, CA: University of California Center for Research and Development in Higher Education.

Clark, D.L. (1985). Emerging paradigms in organizational theory and research. In Y.S. Lincoln (Ed.), *Organizational theory and inquiry: The paradigm revolution* (pp. 43–78). Beverly Hills, CA: Sage.

Clark, D.L., Astuto, T.A., & Kuh, G.D. (in press). Strength of coupling in the organization and operation of colleges and universities. In G.S. Johnston (Ed.), *Research and thought in educational administration*. Lanham, MD: University Press of America.

Cohen, M.D., & March, J.G. (1974). *Leadership and ambiguity: The American college president*. New York: McGraw-Hill.

Cohen, M.D., March, J.G., & Olsen, J.P. (1972). A garbage can model of organizational choice. *Administrative Science Quarterly, 17*(1), 1–25.

Collins, L. (1985). *Fall from grace*. New York: Simon & Schuster.

Conrad, C.F., & Wyer, J.C. (1980). *Liberal education in transition*. Washington, DC: American Association for Higher Education.

Coughlin, E.K. (1985, July 17). The "Crits" v. the legal academy: Arguing a case against the law. *The Chronicle of Higher Education*, 5–6.

Council for the Advancement of Standards for Student Services/Development Programs. (1986). *CAS standards and guidelines for student services/development programs*. Iowa City, IA: American College Testing Program.

Council of Student Personnel Associations in Higher Education. (1975). *Student development services in post-secondary education.* Bowling Green, OH: Bowling Green State University.

Cunningham, D.J. (1986). Good guys and bad guys. *Educational Communication and Technology Journal, 34,* 3–7.

Dutton, T.B., & Rickard, S.T. (1980). Organizing student services. In U. Delworth & G.H. Hanson (Eds.), *Student services: A handbook for the profession* (pp. 386–408). San Francisco: Jossey-Bass.

Erikson, E. (1963). *Childhood and society* (2nd ed.). New York: Norton.

Etzioni, A. (1964). *Modern organizations.* Englewood Cliffs, NJ: Prentice-Hall.

Fenske, R.H. (1980). Current trends. In U. Delworth & G.R. Hanson (Eds.), *Student services: A handbook for the profession* (pp. 45–72). San Francisco: Jossey-Bass.

Ferguson, M. (1980). *The aquarian conspiracy: Personal and social transformation in the 1980's.* Boston: Houghton Mifflin.

Forrest, L., Hotelling, K., & Kuk, L. (1984, June). *The elimination of sexism in university environments.* Paper presented at the Student Development Through Campus Ecology Symposium, Pingree Park, CO.

Foxley, C.H. (Ed.). (1980). Applying management techniques. *New Directions for Student Services,* No. 9. San Francisco: Jossey-Bass.

Friedman, H.S. (1986, May 5). A guide from the perplexed. *Newsweek,* p. 8.

Glaser, B.G., & Strauss, A.L. (1967). *The discovery of grounded theory.* Chicago: Aldine.

Gribbin, J. (1984). *In search of Schrodinger's cat.* New York: Bantam.

Grove, A.S. (1983, October 3). Breaking the chains of command. *Newsweek,* p. 23.

Guba, E.G. (1981). Criteria for assessing the trustworthiness of naturalistic inquiries. *Educational Communication and Technology Journal, 29,* 75–92.

Guba, E.G. (1985). Perspectives on public policy: What can happen as a result of a policy? *Policy Studies Review, 5,* 11–16.

Guba, E.G., & Lincoln, Y.S. (1985, summer). Fourth generation evaluation as an alternative. *Educational Horizons,* 139–141.

Guillen, M.A. (1984, August). The intuitive edge. *Psychology Today,* pp. 68–69.

Hedberg, B., Nystrom, P., & Starbuck, W. (1976). Camping on seesaws: Prescriptions for a self-designing organization. *Administrative Science Quarterly, 21,* 41–65.

Hodgkinson, H.L. (1985). *All one system: Demographics of education, kindergarten through graduate school.* Washington, DC: Institute for Educational Leadership.

Hossler, D. (1984). *Enrollment management.* New York: The College Board.

Howard, G.S. (1985). Can research in the human sciences become more relevant to practice? *Journal of Counseling and Development, 63,* 539–544.

Huff, A.S. (1985). Managerial implications of the emerging paradigm. In Y.S. Lincoln (Ed.), *Organizational theory and inquiry: The paradigm revolution* (pp. 161–183). Beverly Hills, CA: Sage.

Jantsch, E. (1980). *The self-organizing universe.* New York: Pergamon.

Jonas, G. (1982, July). Reality anyone? *Science Digest,* p. 11.

Kanter, R.M. (1983). *The change masters.* New York: Simon & Schuster.

Kilmann, R.H., Saxton, M.J., Serpa, R., & Associates (1986). *Gaining con-*

trol of the corporate culture. San Francisco: Jossey-Bass.

King, J.B. (1986). The three faces of thinking. *Journal of Higher Education, 57,* 78–92.

Klein, D., & Klein, M.E. (1984). *How do you know it's true?* New York: Scribner's Sons.

Knefelkamp, L.L. (1986, April 9). *Keynote address*. Meeting of the American College Personnel Association, New Orleans.

Knefelkamp, L.L., Widick, C., & Parker, C.A. (1978). *Applying new developmental findings: New Directions for Student Services, No. 4*. San Francisco: Jossey-Bass.

Knock, G.H. (Ed.) (1977). *Perspectives on the preparation of student affairs professionals*. Washington, DC: American College Personnel Association.

Kounin, J.S. (1983). *Classrooms: Individuals or behavior settings. Monographs in Teaching and Learning, No. 1*. Bloomington, IN: Indiana University School of Education.

Kuh, G.D. (1981a). *Indices of quality in the undergraduate experience* (AAHE-ERIC/Higher Education Research Report No. 4). Washington, DC: American Association for Higher Education.

Kuh, G.D. (1981b). Beyond student development: Contemporary priorities for student affairs. *NASPA Journal, 18*(1), 29–36.

Kuh, G.D. (1981c). Guiding questions for needs assessments in student affairs. *Journal of the National Association of Women Deans, Administrators and Counselors, 45*(1), 32–38.

Kuh, G.D. (1982). Purposes and principles for needs and assessments in student affairs. *Journal of College Student Personnel, 23,* 202–209.

Kuh, G.D. (1983a). Guiding assumptions about student affairs organizations. In G.D. Kuh (Ed.), *Understanding student affairs organizations: New Directions for Student Services, No. 23* (pp. 15–26). San Francisco: Jossey-Bass.

Kuh, G.D. (1983b). Tactics for understanding and improving student affairs organizations. In G.D. Kuh (Ed.), *Understanding student affairs organizations: New Directions for Student Services, No. 23* (pp. 67–78). San Francisco: Jossey-Bass.

Kuh, G.D. (1984a). A framework for understanding student affairs work. *Journal of College Student Personnel, 25,* 25–31.

Kuh, G.D. (1984b). It's more complicated than that . . . *Journal of College Student Personnel, 25,* 37–38.

Kuh, G.D. (1984c). Suggestions for remaining sane in institutions that don't work the way they're supposed to. *NASPA Journal, 21*(1), 55–61.

Kuh, G.D. (1985). What is extraordinary about ordinary student affairs organizations. *NASPA Journal, 23*(2), 31–43.

Kuh, G.D., Bean, J.P., Bradley, R.K., & Coomes, M.D. (1986a). Contributions of student affairs journals to the college student research. *Journal of College Student Personnel, 27,* 292–304.

Kuh, G.D., Bean, J.P., Bradley, R.K., & Coomes, M.D. (1986b). Is one galaxy enough? *Journal of College Student Personnel, 27,* 311–312.

Kuh, G.D., Bean, J.P., Bradley, R.K., Coomes, M.D., & Hunter, D.E. (1986). Changes in research about college students published in selected journals between 1969 and 1983. *Review of Higher Education, 9,* 177–192.

Kuh, G.D., & Coomes, M.D. (1986). Robert H. Shaffer: The quintessential "do-gooder." *Journal of Counseling and Development, 64,* 614–623.

Kuh, G.D., Dannells, M., Doherty, P., & Ganshaw, T.F. (1977). Student development theory in practice. *NASPA Journal, 16*(2), 48–52.

Kuh, G.D., & McAleenan, A.C. (1986). The future of student affairs work in small colleges. In G.D. Kuh & A.C. McAleenan (Eds.), *Private dreams, shared visions: Student affairs work in small colleges* (pp. 105–119). Columbus, OH: National Association of Student Personnel Administrators.

Kuh, G.D., & Nuss, E.M. (in press). Staying solvent without costing an arm and a leg: Fiscal responsibility in student affairs. In J. Schuh (Ed.), *Financial management for student affairs administrators: A discussion of selected contemporary issues.* Baltimore: ACPA Media.

Kuh, G.D., Shedd, J.D., & Whitt, E.J. (in press). Student affairs and liberal education: Unrecognized common law partners. *Journal of College Student Personnel.*

Kuhn, T.S. (1970). *The structure of scientific revolutions* (2nd ed.). Chicago: University of Chicago Press.

Leemon, T.A. (1972). *The rites of passage in a student culture.* New York: Teachers College Press.

Leontief, W. (1986, January 12). A + B = goodness. *New York Times Book Review*, p. 7.

Lincoln, Y.S. (1986, February). *A future-oriented comment on the state of the profession.* Paper presented at the meeting of the Association for the Study of Higher Education, San Antonio.

Lincoln, Y.S., & Guba, E.G. (1985). *Naturalistic inquiry.* Beverly Hills, CA: Sage.

Lipsky, M. (1980). *Street level bureaucracy: Dilemmas of the individual in public services.* New York: Russell Sage Foundation.

Looft, W.R. (1973). Socialization and personality throughout the life span: A reexamination of contemporary psychological approaches. In P.B. Baltes & K.W. Schaie (Eds.), *Life span developmental psychology: Personality and socialization* (pp. 25–49). New York: Academic Press.

Lucas, C. (1985). Out at the edge: Notes on a paradigm shift. *Journal of Counseling and Development, 64*, 165–172.

Lucas, C.J. (1984). Liberal learning and the humanities: A reaffirmation. *Journal of General Education, 36*, 20–31.

Madison, P. (1969). *Personality development in college.* Reading, MA: Addison-Wesley.

March, J.G. (1972). Model bias in social action. *Review of Educational Research, 42*, 413–429.

March, J.G., & Olsen, J.P. (1976). Organizational choice under ambiguity. In J.G. March & J.P. Olsen (Eds.), *Ambiguity and choice in organizations* (pp. 10–23). Bergen: Universitetsforlaget.

Market gurus jolt the Dow. (1986, July 21). *Newsweek*, p. 30.

Maruyama, M. (1976). Toward cultural symbiosis. In E. Jantsch & C.H. Waddington (Eds.), *Evolution and consciousness: Human systems in transition* (pp. 198–213). Reading, MA: Addison-Wesley.

Masland, A.T. (1985). Organizational culture in the study of higher education. *Review of Higher Education, 8*(2), 157–168.

Miles, M.B., & Huberman, A.M. (1984). *Qualitative data analysis: A sourcebook of new methods.* Beverly Hills, CA: Sage.

Millard, R.M. (1976). *State boards of higher education* (ERIC/Higher Education Research Report No. 4). Washington, DC: American Association for Higher Education.

Miller, R.S. (1985, October). Mind and the new physicis: An interview with Fred Alan Wolf, Ph.D. *Science of Mind*, pp. 11–14, 81–88.

Miller, T.K., & Prince, J.S. (1976). *The future of student affairs.* San Francisco: Jossey-Bass.

Moore, R. (1966). *Niels Bohr: The man, his science, and the world they changed.* New York: Knopf.

Morgan, G. (1980). Paradigms, metaphors, and puzzle solving in organization theory. *Administrative Science Quarterly, 25,* 605–622.

Morgan, G., & Ramirez, R. (1983). Action learning: A holographic metaphor for guiding social change. *Human Relations, 37,* 1–28.

Morrill, W.H., & Hurst, J.C. (Eds.). (1980). *Dimensions for intervention for student development.* New York: Wiley.

Mumford, L. (1956). *The transformations of man.* New York: Harper.

Newton, F.B., & Caple, R.B. (1985). Once the world was flat: Introduction and overview. *Journal of Counseling and Development, 64,* 163–164.

Oblander, F. (1986). *Implementation of student development theory in a student affairs organization: A study of the theory to practice link.* Unpublished doctoral dissertation, Indiana University.

Pagels, H.R. (1985). *Perfect symmetry: The search for the beginning of time.* New York: Simon & Schuster.

Patton, M.Q. (1980). *Qualitative evaluation methods.* Beverly Hills, CA: Sage.

Penney, J. (1972). *Perspective and challenge in college student personnel work.* Springfield, IL: Charles C Thomas.

Perls, F. (1969). *Gestalt therapy verbatim.* New York: Bantam.

Perrow, C. (1981). Disintegrating social sciences. *New York University Education Quarterly, 22*(2), 2–9.

Perry, W., Jr. (1970). *Forms of intellectual and ethical development in the college years: A scheme.* New York: Holt, Rinehart and Winston.

Peters, T.J., & Waterman, R.H., Jr. (1982). *In search of excellence: Lessons from America's best run companies.* New York: Harper & Row.

Pondy, L.R. (1978). Leadership as a language game. In M.W. McCall, Jr., & M.M. Lombardo (Eds.), *Leadership: Where else can we go?* (pp. 87–101). Durham, NC: Duke University Press.

Pribram, K.H. (1977). Some comments on the nature of the perceived universe. In R. Shaw & J. Bransford (Eds.). *Perceiving, acting, and knowing.* New York: Wiley.

Prigogine, I., & Stengers, I. (1984). *Order out of chaos.* New York: Bantam.

Reason, P., & Rowan, J. (1981). On making sense. In P. Reason and J. Rowan (Eds.), *Human inquiry: A sourcebook of new paradigm research* (pp. 113–137). New York: Wiley.

Reinharz, S. (1981). Implementing new paradigm research: A model for training and practice. In P. Reason & J. Rowan (Eds.), *Human inquiry: A sourcebook of new paradigm research* (pp. 415–436). New York: Wiley.

Rentz, A.L. (1976). A triadic model master's program in student development. *Journal of College Student Personnel, 17,* 453–458.

Rodgers, R.F. (1977). Student personnel work as social intervention. In G.H. Knock (Ed.), *Perspectives on the preparation of student affairs professionals* (pp. 12–34). Washington, DC: American College Personnel Association.

Rodgers, R.F. (1983). Using theory in practice. In T.K. Miller, R.B. Winston, & W.R. Mendenhall (Eds.), *Administration and leadership in student affairs: Actualizing student development in higher education* (pp. 111–144). Muncie, IN: Accelerated Development.

Rogers, C.R. (1951). *Client-centered therapy.* Boston: Houghton Mifflin.

Rogers, C.R. (1961). *On becoming a person.* Boston: Houghton Mifflin.

Rogers, C.R. (1970). *On encounter groups.* New York: Harper & Row.

Sanford, R.N. (1962). The developmental status of the freshman. In R.N. Sanford (Ed.), *The American college* (pp. 253–282). New York: Wiley.

Sawada, D., & Caley, M. (1985). Dissipative structures: New metaphors for becoming in education. *Educational Researcher, 14*(3), 13–19.

Scarr, S. (1985). Constructing, psychology: Making facts and fables for our times. *American Psychologist, 40*(5), 499–512.

Schein, E.H. (1985). *Organizational culture and leadership: A dynamic view.* San Francisco: Jossey-Bass.

Schlossberg, N.K. (1981). A model for analyzing human adaptation to transition. *Counseling Psychologist, 9*(2), 2–18.

Schroeder, C.C. (1986). President's communiqué. *ACPA Developments, 13*(3), 1, 13, 18.

Schroeder, C.C., Nicholls, G.E., & Kuh, G.D. (1983). Exploring the rain forest: Testing assumptions and taking risks. In G.D. Kuh (Ed.), *Understanding student affairs organizations: New Directions for Student Services, No. 23* (pp. 51–65). San Francisco: Jossey-Bass.

Schuh, J.H., & Laverty, M. (1983). The perceived long-term effect of holding a significant student leadership position. *Journal of College Student Personnel, 24,* 28–32.

Schwartz, P., & Ogilvy, J. (1979). *The emergent paradigm: Changing patterns of thought and belief* (Analytical Report No. 7, Values and Lifestyles Program). Menlo Park, CA: SRI International.

Sergiovanni, T.J. (1984a). Expanding conceptions of inquiry and practice in supervision and evaluation. *Educational Evaluation and Policy Analysis, 6,* 355–365.

Sergiovanni, T.J. (1984b). Cultural and competing perspectives in administrative theory and practice. In T.J. Sergiovanni & J.E. Corbally (Eds.), *Leadership and organizational culture: New perspectives on administrative theory and practice* (pp. 1–12). Urbana: University of Illinois Press.

Sergiovanni, T.J. (1984c). Leadership as cultural expression. In T.J. Sergiovanni & J.E. Corbally (Eds.), *Leadership and organizational culture: New perspectives on administrative theory and practice* (pp. 105–114). Urbana: University of Illinois Press.

Siegal, S. (1956). *Non-parametric statistics for the behavioral sciences.* New York: McGraw-Hill.

Skrtic, T.M. (1985). Doing naturalistic research into educational organizations. In Y.S. Lincoln (Ed.), *Organizational theory and inquiry: The paradigm revolution.* Beverly Hills, CA: Sage.

Spooner, S.E. (1979). Preparing the student development specialist: the process-outcome model applied. *Journal of College Student Personnel, 20,* 45–53.

Stamatakos, L.C. (1981). Student affairs progress toward professionalism: Recommendations for action—Part I. *Journal of College Student Personnel, 22,* 197–207.

Stamatakos, L.C., & Rogers, R. (1984). Student affairs: A profession in need of a philosophy. *Journal of College Student Personnel, 25,* 400–411.

Strange, C.C. (1983). Traditional perspectives on student affairs organizations. In G.D. Kuh (Ed.), *Understanding student affairs organizations: New Directions for Student Services, No. 23* (pp. 5–13). San Francisco: Jossey-Bass.

Strange, C.C., & Contomanolis, E. (1983). Knowledge perceptions of human development theory among student development master's students. *Journal of College Student Personnel, 24,* 197–201.

Toffler, A. (1984). Foreword: Science and change. In I. Prigogine & I. Stengers, *Order out of chaos* (pp. xi–xxvi). New York: Bantam.

Tranel, D.D. (1981). A lesson from the physicists. *Personnel and Guidance Journal, 59,* 425–429.

Tuckman, B.W. (1978). *Conducting educational research* (2nd ed.). New York: Harcourt Brace Jovanovich.

Weick, K.E. (1976). Educational organizations as loosely coupled systems. *Administrative Science Quarterly, 21*, 1–18.

Weick, K.E. (1979). *The social psychology of organizing.* (2nd ed.). Reading, MA: Addison-Wesley.

Weick, K.E. (1982). Administering education in loosely coupled schools. *Phi Delta Kappan, 62*, 673–676.

Weick, K.E. (1985). Sources of order in underorganized systems: Themes in recent organizational theory. In Y.S. Lincoln (Ed.), *Organizational theory and inquiry: The paradigm revolution*. Beverly Hills, CA: Sage.

Whetten, D.A. (1984). Effective administrators: Good management on the college campus. *Change, 16*(8), 38–43.

White, R.W. (1966). *Lives in progress* (2nd ed.). New York: Holt, Rinehart and Winston.

Winkler, K.J. (1985, June 26). Questioning the science in social science, scholars signal a 'turn to interpretation.' *The Chronicle of Higher Education*, pp. 5–6.

Winkler, K.J. (1985, August 7). Historians fail to explain science to laymen, scholar says. *The Chronicle of Higher Education*, p. 7.

Winkler, K.J. (1986, January 8). A historian criticizes value-free scholarship, cites need for moral judgment in research. *The Chronicle of Higher Education*, pp. 10–11.

Yin, R.K. (1984). *Case study research: Design and methods*. Beverly Hills, CA: Sage.

Zukav, G. (1980). *The dancing Wu Li masters: An overview of the new physics*. New York: Bantam Books.

ANNOTATED BIBLIOGRAPHY

The following annotations are representative of ideas congenial to the emergent paradigm. Some of these readings are more evocative than others; some are easier to understand than others. For some entries, we have estimated the level of difficulty and complexity of the presentation.

Argyris, C., & Schon, D.A. (1978). *Organizational learning: A theory of action perspective.* Reading, MA: Addison-Wesley.

The authors describe how organizations learn or fail to learn by distinguishing three types of organizational learning: (a) "single-loop" learning is the detection and correction of organizational error that permits the organization to carry on present policies and practices with minimal disruption; (b) "double-loop" learning occurs when organizational error is detected and corrected in ways that surface and challenge underlying norms, values, policies, and objectives; (c) "deutero-learning" is the process of inquiry into the learning system by which an organization detects and corrects its errors. The authors provide five case studies to illustrate how individuals can develop theories of action conducive to fostering organizational learning and renewal.

Capra, F. (1982). *The turning point: Science, society, and the rising culture.* New York: Simon & Schuster.

Capra's primary thesis is that the major crises facing the world are, in fact, different aspects of one crisis: a crisis of perception, of trying to apply a set of anachronistic assumptions (i.e., the mechanistic paradigm of Cartesian-Newtonian science) to a dynamic, indeterminate, and interdependent world. Traditional ways of thinking are simply inadequate to describe and understand present phenomena.

There is hope, however. During the 20th century, dramatic changes in concepts in physics have led to equally dramatic changes in world views across disciplines and within individuals. These changes represent a shift from Cartesian-Newtonian mechanism to an ecological, holistic view, a view that is "similar to the views of mystics of all ages and traditions" (p. 15).

Evidence of this paradigm shift can be seen in recent social and political movements, in the integration of Western and Eastern approaches in psychology, increasing emphasis on spirituality, and on developing ecological and feminist perspectives. The apparent trend toward political, social, and religious conservatism can be interpreted as a defensive response on the part of dominant institutions. But, "as the turning point approaches, the realization that evolutionary changes of this magnitude cannot be prevented by short-term political activities provides our strongest hope for the future" (p. 419).

Of the numerous paperbacks on this topic, this is one of the best. However, if you're not prepared for a primer in physics, this—like the Zukav volume described later—may seem dense, but worth the effort.

Cohen, M.D., & March, J.G. (1974). *Leadership and ambiguity: The American college president.* New York: McGraw-Hill.

Cohen and March examine the college presidency, using a variety of empirical and theoretical frameworks, with the aim of describing ways in which presidents can be effective leaders despite the ambiguity inherent in IHEs. The American college or university is a prototypical organized anarchy: "It does not know what it is doing. Its goals are either vague or in dispute. Its technology is familiar, but not understood. Its major participants wander in and out of the organization" (p. 3). Thus, traditional theories of organizing that emphasize coordination and control and assume clear goals do not provide very useful guidance for college presidents.

The authors offer ways of thinking about leadership and organizations compatible with the realities of contemporary IHEs: alternative metaphors of leadership, alternative models of choice (e.g, the "garbage can"), tactics for leadership in organized anarchies, and a description— and a plea for adopting—a technology of foolishness.

This volume is a prescient, classic entry to the higher education literature, and is well worth reading.

Ferguson, M. (1980). *The aquarian conspiracy: Personal and social transformation in the 1980's.* Los Angeles: J.P. Tarcher.

The conspiracy to which Ferguson refers is a conspiracy for a new human agenda demanded by the inadequacy of old assumptions for making meaning in today's world. The conspiracy is fueled by the social implications of recent scientific research into human capacities and human nature, and in efforts to experiment with expanding consciousness and awareness. Aquarian conspirators propose a new paradigm that is inherently paradoxical: pragmatic yet transcendental, emphasizing interdependence and individuality, and valuing mystery as well as enlightenment.

Ferguson describes a process of personal and cultural change, exhibited in transformations in knowledge, politics, health and healing, learning, spirituality, human relationships, values, and vocation. These transformations support and reflect a fundamentally altered view of human and social potential: the individual as autonomous steward of her or his own resources, yet embedded in nature and an interconnected global village.

Kanter, R.M. (1983). *The change masters.* New York: Simon & Schuster.

Using 10 extensive case studies of companies and research data from an additional 70 organizations, Kanter identified qualities associated with effective and ineffective organizations. By comparing organizational design factors characteristic of the 1890–1920 period with the design factors typical of 1960–1980, the author suggests that American organizations are in the midst of a "transforming era" that demands changes in practices and ways of thinking about organizing. For example, organizations that encourage innovation are depicted as integrative whereas organizations that seem to inhibit innovation are highly segmented. Kanter describes the conditions for innovation and the evolution of innovations through an organization and suggests ways that organizations can be transformed through encouraging and supporting innovation.

Kanter's illustrations are rich; emergent paradigm concepts are introduced but are not labeled as such. We think you will find her suggestions practical and useful.

Kuh, G.D. (Ed.). (1983). *Understanding student affairs organizations: New Directions for Student Services, No. 23*. San Francisco: Jossey-Bass.

When student affairs organizations do not work as expected, perhaps we should reexamine our expectations rather than attempting to "fix" the organization. The contributors to this source book suggest that expectations are often based on assumptions of rationality, predictability, and order. Linked to these assumptions are a number of myths about student affairs organizations including: that shared a priori goals are important and necessary for directing activities and behavior; that decision making can, and should, be rational; that rewards and sanctions are merit-based; and that educational organizations are tightly coupled systems.

The contributors encourage the use of multiple perspectives for interpreting what goes on in student affairs organizations, so that more purposeful and effective actions can be implemented. Alternative ways (organized anarchy, incentive exchange, loose coupling) of looking at and understanding behavior in student affairs organizations are examined and tactics are provided for expanding expectations and assumptions for organizational processes, including arational metaphors for planning.

Kuhn, T.S. (1970). *The structure of scientific revolutions* (2nd ed.). Chicago: University of Chicago Press.

Described as a "landmark in intellectual history," Kuhn's work is one of the best known harbingers of the evolution from conventional paradigm, normal science ways of knowing and discovering knowledge to a qualitatively different paradigm or world view. Kuhn uses analytical methods from the philosophy and history of science to identify anomalies or disjuncts between theory and research compatible with positivist-based theory and research. He analyzes the confluence of factors that contributed to "the scientific revolution," or shift from a conventional to emergent paradigm.

The writing is generally clear and interesting. One possible source of confusion is the multiple meanings Kuhn attributes to the term *paradigm*; at least 23 different usages appear in the volume.

Lincoln, Y.S. (Ed.). (1985). *Organizational theory and inquiry: The paradigm revolution*. Beverly Hills, CA: Sage.

The contributors examine two significant paradigm shifts; the first is substantive and disciplinary—organizational theory—and the second is methodological and epistemological—how we investigate and accumulate knowledge about the world. These shifts are simultaneous and interrelated; assumptions and understandings about organizing are inextricably related to the ways in which organizations are studied and interpreted.

Part 1 sets a context for the shift in paradigms. The history of orthodox organizational theory is presented and the axioms of orthodox and naturalistic research paradigms are described. Part 2 provides an explication of New Story concepts, including new metaphors for organizing and implications of naturalistic inquiry axioms. In part 3, the contributors discuss the significance of new paradigm beliefs for knowledge and understanding obtained through research.

Lincoln, Y.S., & Guba, E.G. (1985). *Naturalistic inquiry*. Beverly Hills: Sage.

In the words of the authors, this volume proposes a heresy: that the positivist inquiry paradigm is inadequate for studying and understanding human behavior. Positivism seeks a single reality, restricts the purposes of research to prediction and control, and, as a consequence, disregards the humanness of the persons studied.

Naturalistic inquiry assumes multiple realities and interdependence between knower and known, acknowledges time-, context-, and value-boundedness of inquiry, and assumes mutual simultaneous shaping among people (including the inquirer) and events. Lincoln and Guba provide a detailed and clear description of the process of naturalistic inquiry, enabling (and encouraging) the reader to explore first-hand the possibilities of this alternative paradigm for better understanding of human behavior.

Newton, F.B., & Caple, R.B. (Eds.). (1985). Paradigm shifts: Considerations for practice. *Journal of Counseling and Development, 64*(3).

Over time, world views come to represent reality (not perception), provide a sense of common meanings and mechanisms for understanding, and tend to discourage consideration of competing world views or interpretive frameworks. World views change only after a sufficient amount of data are accumulated that cannot be reconciled with the world view in use. The period of transition between world views is a period of confusion, in which new rules, new paths, new questions, and new answers must be sought.

This special issue of the *Journal of Counseling and Development* is a collection of insights formulated to help cope during the transition. The current shift in world views is described, with an emphasis on new psychological thrusts and their significance for counseling theory and practice. In the section devoted to reconstructing counseling theory, articles are included that address the self-organization paradigm, quantum theory and the person-centered approach, and applications of Gilligan's theory of sex-role development to counseling. In the discussion of changes in counseling practice, topics include dream therapy, the role of metaphors in psychological development, learning styles, psychological resonance, methods for extending consciousness, and transcendental meditation.

Prigogine, I., & Stengers, I. (1984). *Order out of chaos*. New York: Bantam.

Drawing on examples from the natural and physical sciences, the authors demonstrate that most systems in the physical universe (including IHEs and people) are open (i.e., an entity is in constant flux and change connected to and influenced by the surrounding context). Interactions of open systems with elements in the environment are characterized more by disequilibrium and disorder than a basic tendency to maintain or return to stability and order. Organisms have the capacity to self-organize, or to evolve from what may seem to be a state of chaos or disorganization to more sophisticated or complicated levels of development or organization. Neither the movement to a different evolutionary stage or form nor the characteristics of the new form can be predicted or anticipated. This view of evolutionary change is in stark contrast to interpretations of development or change characteristic of a mechanistic, deterministic world in which movement was thought to be a function of casual events connected in a linear, sequential manner.

This book is difficult reading; the foreword by Alvin Toffler is quite insightful and must be read before plunging into the text.

Reason, P., & Rowan, J. (Eds.). (1981). *Human inquiry: A sourcebook of new paradigm research.* London: Wiley.

A variety of works are presented that address the need for, and offer approaches to, a new paradigm for research about human beings. Limitations of conventional inquiry in studying people are explored and include emphases on objectivity and detachment, on quantification and measurement, and on isolation and separation of person from context. New paradigm research is described as "objectively subjective"—the systematic and rigorous pursuit of truth that also appreciates experience and intuition, provides for collaboration between researcher and respondent, and acknowledges as appropriate the influence of perceptions and context of the inquirer and subject of inquiry on research outcomes. Some of the alternative approaches encompassed here within the new inquiry paradigm are not necessarily new, including humanistic psychology, action research, feminist scholarship, phenomenology, and illuminative evaluation. In the words of Reason and Rowan, "here is another way of doing research. Try it."

Schein, E.H. (1985). *Organizational culture and leadership: A dynamic view.* San Francisco: Jossey-Bass.

The purpose of this book is twofold: (a) to define the concept of organizational culture, and (b) to demonstrate the interconnectedness of organizational culture and organizational leadership. Organizational culture is a pattern of basic shared assumptions and beliefs that are learned responses to organizational problems of internal integration and external adaptation. Schein asserts the possibility that "the only thing of real importance that leaders do is create and manage culture" (p. 2).

Topics treated include the effects of culture on organizational life, the importance of studying culture, means to find and understand organizational assumptions, mechanisms by which leaders form and maintain culture, and mechanisms for cultural change and organizational evolution. This work reflects an interdisciplinary view of organizations and leadership, drawing from sociology, psychology, and learning theory—and is intended for use by practitioners as well as theorists. Both will be informed by Schein's observations.

Schwartz, P., & Olgilvy, J. (1979). *The emergent paradigm: Changing patterns of thought and belief.* Analytical Report No. 7, Values and Lifestyles Program. Menlo Park, CA: SRI International.

The major assertion of this report is that we are between stories; that is, a transition is taking place between world views or paradigms—"a fundamental shift in the basic beliefs and assumptions about the nature of things and the human condition is going on." To support the claim of the emergence of a qualitatively different world view or paradigm, the authors draw on examples of research and thought from the following disciplines: physics, chemistry, brain theory, mathematics, biology, philosophy, political theory, linguistics, consciousness, psychology, religion, and the arts. Patterns of change of particular interest include the concept of order, the fundamental interconnectedness among parts of any whole (e.g., society, IHEs, family personality), and challenges to objectivity and truth. The authors suggest implications of the emergent paradigm and conclude with the proposition that emergent paradigm qualities are more like aesthetics than like science.

This is an excellent, compelling overview of how the emergent paradigm is being manifested in various fields. The article has not been widely distributed (except on the academic black market) as it was commissioned for proprietary purposes by a consortium of manufacturers.

Weick, K.E. (1979). *The social psychology of organizing* (2nd ed.). Reading, MA: Addison-Wesley.

Weick develops an organizational epistemology, exploring and assessing the nature, origins, and limits of organizational knowledge, that is, how organizations perceive and understand themselves and their environments. Weick's primary focus is organizational processes, examined from the perspective of nonorthodox organizational theory, not as defined in orthodox prescriptions (e.g., expectations for coordination, control, planning, production). "The substance of organizing . . . is interlocked behaviors" (p. 4), a confluence of procedures, behaviors, puzzles, and interpretations. Elements of nonorthodox interpretations of organizing include equivocal information, sense-making activities, created realities, ambivalence toward experience, adaptability, dense and circular causal chains, enacted limitations, and networks of self-regulating causal links. Weick offers nonorthodox tactics for thinking about organizing so that managers "can see their circumstances more richly" (p. 240), and better understand their organization.

This volume is a classic in organizational theory. The novice as well as the seasoned administrator will appreciate the depth and richness of Weick's insights into behavior in the organizational context.

Zukav, G. (1979). *The dancing Wu Li masters*. New York: Morrow.

This book provides an introduction to new physics for the nonphysicist. With the caveat "be gentle with yourself as you read" (xxix), Zukav sets out on a journey through quantum mechanics interspersed with Eastern philosophy; "Wu Li" is a term used in Taiwan for the study of physics and means "patterns of organic energy" as well as "nonsense," "enlightenment," and "my way."

Quantum mechanics is the study of the motion of subatomic bits and pieces (quanta) of nature (e.g., photons, electrons). Discoveries within the subatomic realm have led some physicists (and others) to conclude that "old physics"—and old world views—are inadequate to explain what we see. Heisenberg's uncertainty principle is an example of new ways of looking at the world offered by new physics. Heisenberg discovered that it was impossible to know simultaneously the position and the momentum of a particle; one must choose which will be known. The choice of experiment determines what will be observed. It follows, then, that the process of observation affects what is observed, which, in turn, calls into question the concept of objectivity. "Reality" is what we make it. Thus, Zukav concludes, "if the new physics has led us anywhere, it is back to ourselves, which, of course, is the only place we could go" (p. 114).

GLOSSARY

Action learning Questioning and responding with reflective action to learned or traditional assumptions, beliefs, and policies that may be dysfunctional at a given stage of an organization's evolution. Action learning requires that persons challenge established policies and practices with experimental activities to create a more open, responsive self-organizing environment (chapter 5).

"Believing is seeing" An aphorism that underscores the relationship between expectations and beliefs and subsequent interpretations of what is observed; one sees what one expects to see or believes is there. The obverse of "seeing is believing" (preface, chapter 2).

Bifurcation point The demarcation between what seems to be a chaotic state of affairs and a new, reordered form of organization or personality. Reordering is a consequence of the spontaneous change that can occur in a dissipative structure with open system characteristics (chapters 2–4).

Causal scientism See logical positivism.

Complementarity principle A quantum mechanics principle that holds that matter at the subatomic level exhibits contradictory tendencies. For example, light can take on properties of and behave like particles or like waves (chapter 1).

Constructed reality An individual's view or interpretation of what is. Events have no meaning outside of the context in which they are observed, so reality—what happened how, when and by whom—must be constructed by each observer or participant in the event. In the emergent paradigm, multiple realities are acknowledged and are treated as valid. Reality can also be socially constructed, the result of negotiations among individual perspectives and interpretations (chapters 2, 3, 5, 6).

Conventional paradigm A set of assumptions and beliefs about the nature of the physical world dating from Copernicus and Newton to the present. In this dominant world view, a single reality exists that can be discovered. The world is like a machine, the parts of which are identifiable and have a predictable, sequential relationship with one another.

Dissipative structure An open system (e.g., a human being, a student affairs division, an institution of higher education) capable of both spontaneous, evolutionary (second-order) change and incremental, seemingly patterned, orderly development (first-order change). External stimulus is not necessary for change to occur. Dissipative structures have the capacity to become reordered or reintegrated following a period of chaos, although the characteristics of the reordered state cannot be predicted (chapters 2–4).

Double looping   The ability to go beyond detecting and correcting problems and errors in previously defined issues and courses of action to challenge extant values, assumptions, policies, and practices; similar to action learning (chapter 5).

Ecology   A behavior setting (such as an institution of higher education) made up of physical, cultural, social, and economic relational networks that are both internal and external to the setting. The mutual influence of these networks creates what happens within the behavior setting.

Emergent paradigm   A set of assumptions and beliefs that encompasses ideas and concepts from the conventional paradigm, but also redefines ways in which experiences are interpreted and understood. The emergent paradigm is synonymous with the new world or New Story. New Story qualities of mutual shaping, multiple realities, holonomy, heterarchy, indeterminacy, and morphogenesis are described and contrasted with conventional qualities in chapter 2.

Hermeneutics   The science or art of interpretation, usually associated with the humanities—particularly biblical studies (see chapters 4 and 7 for applications to student affairs).

Heterarchy   The emergent paradigm counterpart to hierarchy. In the conventional world view, knowledge, authority, and responsibility were thought to be arranged hierarchically; that is people with seniority or who held positions at or near the head of an organization or group (family, club, etc.) were expected to have superior knowledge and provide answers, decisions, and leadership. Heterarchy implies that all persons in an organization or group have something of importance to contribute to decisions and that persons closest to the event or behavior under consideration are in the best position to provide information about the nature, meaning, and implications of the event. Asymmetrical power relationships are viewed as temporary (chapter 2).

Holonomy   Adapted from the holographic principle wherein the whole can be reconstructed from any part, holonomy connotes an interconnectedness among what may appear to be disparate events and elements. All actions or events are connected in some way but not necessarily in ways that can be seen, documented, or clearly understood (chapter 2).

Indeterminacy   A characteristic of the physical world according to which events cannot be predicted because the reciprocal influence among elements—and, hence, causes and effects—are impossible to determine exactly. The principle of indeterminacy (also called the uncertainty principle) is often attributed to Werner Heisenberg, who proved it was impossible to measure precisely, at any given instant, both the velocity and position of an electron because the act of observing influences the process of measurement (chapters 1, 2).

Logical positivism   An inquiry paradigm consistent with the conventional world view in which a single reality, objectivity, clear cause and effect linkages, and generalizability are valued. Experimental or quantitative methods are preferred by logical positivists, although qualitative methods can be used (chapter 6).

Morphogenesis   Change that results from spontaneous and cumulative incremental changes and that leads to new and unanticipated outcomes or structures (chapters 2–5).

Multiple realities   According to the conventional world view, a single reality can be discovered. In the emergent paradigm, each individual constructs his or her own meaning of an experience. By acknowledging the legitimacy of the perceptions of all, the emergent paradigm is host to multiple and sometimes conflicting interpretations of the same event. Within the conventional paradigm, one would seek the "truth" from among competing perspectives (chapters 1, 2, 4–6).

Mutual shaping   People, events, and processes influence one another in ways that affect outcomes, but also in ways that prohibit linking specific causes with specific effects. The converse of linear causality, a concept of the conventional paradigm (chapters 2, 4–7).

Naturalistic inquiry   An inquiry paradigm consistent with the qualities of the emergent world view and one that assumes subjectivity, holism, mutual simultaneous shaping, and context-bound meanings. Naturalism uses tacit knowledge and a human instrument and qualitative methods as inquiry tools, and seeks to develop an insider's viewpoint (chapters 6, 7).

New Story   See emergent paradigm.

Nonorthodox organizational theory   Organizational theory that is compatible with emergent paradigm assumptions. Nonorthodox organizational theory posits that (a) organizational life is ambiguous, (b) intentions and actions are loosely coupled, and (c) organizational and individual preferences tend to be problematic and often conflictual. Nonorthodox concepts of organizing include loose coupling, culture, emergent structures and designs, and retrospective planning (chapters 2, 5).

Normal science   See logical positivism.

Objectivity The proposition that reality is external to or independent of the mind.

Old Story See conventional paradigm.

Orthodox organizational theory Organizational theory consistent with the traditional, bureaucratic assumptions about organizational behavior postulated by Weber. Assumptions include (a) expertise, control, and authority are vested in and exercised by superordinates; (b) unit goals and the means to attain them are clear, shared, and give direction to organizational outcomes; (c) intentions are directly linked to action; and (d) hierarchical structures are normal and necessary. Contrast to nonorthodox theory above (chapters 2, 5).

Paradigm An ordered set of understandings. In this context, paradigm refers to the set of pervasive beliefs and assumptions that govern understanding of fundamental events in the world (chapter 1).

Perspectival An emergent paradigm quality that posits that understanding is context-bound. The meanings of an event or observation can only be understood and appreciated within the context in which the observation or event occurred and within the frame of reference of the observer (chapters 1, 2, 6).

Phenomenology The study and appreciation of events as they appear and are interpreted by an observer.

Quantum mechanics Applications of quantum theory to examine behavior in the physical world at the atomic, and particularly, the subatomic level. Extensions of quantum mechanics have suggested that the universe is constantly evolving and that, although the behavior of particles at the subatomic level cannot be predicted with certainty, the behavior of all elements are somehow related although not necessarily in causal ways (chapter 1).

Self-organization theory The theoretical framework that explains the behavior of open system dissipative structures (Bertalanffy, 1968) that have the capacity to evolve from chaos and disorder into more differentiated, reordered state (Prigogine & Stengers, 1984) (chapters 2–4).

Single looping An approach to problem resolution and policy development that relies on error detection and correction of problems in the context of previously defined courses of action; tinkering and adjusting rather than questioning and changing (chapter 5).

Uncertainty principle See indeterminacy.

Yang Characteristics of nature and humans traditionally associated with men, such as independence, calculation, cognition, aloofness, objectivity, and power. Considered the antithesis of yin.

Yin Characteristics of nature and humans traditionally associated with women, such as nurturance, affect, compassion, intuition, patience, and subjectivity. Considered the antithesis of yang.